ACTIVITIES

Thinking & Learning Skills

AGES 7-11

MIKE FLEETHAM

Author
Mike Fleetham

Development Editor
Kate Pedlar

Editor
Caroline Carless

Project Editor
Fabia Lewis

Series Designers
Anthony Long and
Joy Monkhouse

Designer
Allison Parry

Illustrations
Moreno Chiacchiera

The publishers would like to thank:
Jonathan Le Fevre for permission to use his idea for the thinking board.
Goldsmith Infant School, Portsmouth for permission to use photographs taken at the school.

Author's dedications:
I would like to dedicate this book to Charlie and Edward Hale – two very creative chaps. I would also like to offer my special thanks to my family – for always being there and for believing in me – and Andrew Pearce, Critical Skills Programme Manager for Wales, for sharing ideas, inspiration and encouragement. (MF)

Published by Scholastic Ltd,
Book End,
Range Road,
Witney,
Oxfordshire OX29 0YD

www.scholastic.co.uk

Text © 2008 Mike Fleetham
© 2008 Scholastic Ltd

Designed using Adobe Indesign

Printed in China through Golden Cup Printing Services

2 3 4 5 6 7 8 9   0 1 2 3 4 5 6 7

British Library Cataloguing-in-Publication Data

A catalogue record for this book is available from the British Library.

ISBN 978-1407-10006-7

The rights of Mike Fleetham to be identified as the author of this work have been asserted by him in accordance with the Copyright, Designs and Patents Act 1988.

Contents

4 Introduction

Chapter One:

Get thinking; get learning!

8 Brain gain

10 Learner's recipe

12 Most wanted (1)

14 Most wanted (2)

16 Don't worry; be happy!

18 Le Fevre Plus teaching board

20 Apollo thinking

Chapter Two:

Thinking, learning and literacy

28 The magic writing mat

30 Multi-metaphor me

32 Dear Sir/Madam...

34 MI library

36 Fairy tale jigsaw

38 Distant voices

Chapter Three:

Thinking, learning, numeracy and science

48 Creative Venn

50 Oh dear! What can the matter be?

52 What next?

54 Tables speed dating

56 Scream Park

58 Chemical plant

60 Shapeshifter Betty

Chapter Four:

Thinking, learning and the humanities

68 So what if...

70 Time tunnel

72 Ultimate town planner

Chapter Five:

Thinking, learning and the creative arts

76 What's the score?

78 Class profile

80 Creative meditation

82 Learning tableau

84 Painting by numbers

Chapter Six:

Thinking, learning and PE

90 Bigger, better all-team rounders

92 Virtual helpers

Introduction

Why teach the skills of thinking and learning?

Success in life and learning now depends as much on having the right skills as it does on knowing the right things. Educational experts and business people such as Sir Ken Robinson, Professor Howard Gardner and Stan Shih link a country's future success to its workforce's ability to think, learn and create. Therefore, our young children need opportunities to develop these skills from the moment they start school, not as an afterthought just before they begin work. The creative activities in this book provide an introduction to the skills that the 21st century will demand of them.

Categorising the skills of thinking and learning

There are many, many ways to categorise the skills of thinking and learning. The 30 activities in this book all use a straightforward model with eight main skills. These skills are not exclusive, but are illustrative of the important features of thinking and learning:

These eight main skills can be split into various sub-skills, such as:

● Managing thoughts: handling facts and ideas by sorting, sequencing, remembering, finding out, comparing and arranging.

● Creating thoughts: having new thoughts and ideas through synthesising, creating and innovating.

● Using thoughts: applying facts, thoughts and ideas by evaluating, problem-solving, questioning, enquiring, critical thinking and making decisions.

● Thinking about thinking: reflecting on the management, creation and use of thoughts via the processes of metacognition, planning thinking, monitoring thinking and evaluating thinking.

● Collaboration: learning effectively with others through teamwork, co-operating, leading and organising.

● Independence: learning alone and developing the skills of self-motivation, taking risks, persevering, enterprise and handling change.

● Engagement: defining learning preferences and subject interest by looking

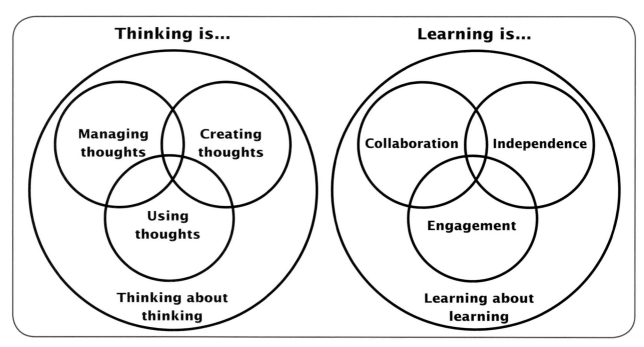

at learning styles, learning readiness, intelligence profiles, preferred subjects and dreams.

● Learning about learning: assessing learning through self-knowledge, reflecting on the learning process and target setting. The diagram on page 4 shows that the three central skills in the 'Thinking' half of the diagram overlap each other and are surrounded by the fourth skill, 'Thinking about thinking'. The 'Learning' half of the diagram is organised in the same way to show how everything fits together. The boundaries between all the skills and sub-skills are not always clear-cut so there will inevitably be some overlap between the two halves.

Variety of skills

Rather than target a single main skill in each activity in this book, opportunities are provided for children to experience a variety of the sub-skills. After all, this is how the real world works: we are required to use multiple skills to achieve an end product. The full range of thinking and learning skills is covered across the 30 activities, thus regular inclusion of these creative activities in teaching sessions over a year will guarantee full skill coverage. Children will get many chances to develop each skill area and to build up their experience at a pace which suits them. Share your successes with these activities at www.thinkingclassroom.co.uk (and download addtional ones).

How to use this book

This book can be used on its own or with its companion (*Creative Activities: Thinking and Learning Skills 5–7*) to provide coverage right across the primary age and ability range. The skills introduced here are developed from the activities featured in the 5–7 book. Children who need support may benefit from starting with the 5–7 activities. As far as possible, the contexts have been chosen to suit all ages from 5 to 11.

© Derek Cooknell

How to use the activities in this book

Each activity takes only one or two teaching sessions and combines a range of creative learning skills with important curriculum objectives, allowing you to develop your children's thinking and learning skills alongside curriculum subjects. The activities are described clearly and include instructions on how to set up and run each activity and evaluate the outcome at the end. They are divided into five curriculum-linked chapters (2–6) with Chapter 1 introducing thinking and learning skills. Consider using the first chapter before any of the others – these activities prepare children to develop their thinking and learning skills before the introduction of curriculum-linked tasks. The introduction to each chapter provides some background information. Then each activity follows the same format: Setting the context, The challenge, Objectives, You will need, Preparation, What to do, Drawing together, Support and Extension.

Objectives

These cover curriculum areas as well as thinking and learning skills. For example: a curriculum objective could be to know number bonds to 20. For the same task, the learning skill objective could be to work successfully in a group of three, while the thinking skill objective could be to compare and sort numbers by set criteria.

Preparation

This section includes anything that needs to be done before the lesson: this might include trying out an activity beforehand or making sample products for children to see before embarking on a task. In some activities there is the opportunity for role play as part of an imaginary scenario. Consider how you would do this, whether you might dress up yourself or invite another adult to take on the role.

What to do

This is a step-by-step explanation of how to carry out the activity and enable the children to solve the problem, often involving an imaginary context introduced at the beginning of the lesson. It is your guide for delivering the activity and includes questions and directions for the children. Children may be required to work individually, in pairs or in groups.

Drawing together

Directions for the plenary session include information to support peer assessment and assessment for learning. Some activities encourage you to devise a 'Levels of success' assessment grid with the class (see example below). As more activities are experienced it is important to involve all children in developing their own success grids or assessment tables: this can take place where 'Levels of success' charts are not provided. Just before the children begin a main task, ask them what a fantastic result would look and sound like; what one that was nearly there would look and sound like and what one that needed more effort would look and sound like. Record the children's answers and refer to them during and after the task.

Differentiation

Ideas for supporting and extending children are both given in terms of the curriculum objectives and the thinking and learning skills required for each task.

Photocopiable pages

Many of the activities come with photocopiable resources. These can be found at the end of each chapter and may be photocopied for use in the classroom. More information on this book can be found at www.thinkingclassroom. co.uk.

Example of a 'Levels of success' chart

Not there yet ☆	Nearly there ☆☆	Fantastic ☆☆☆
✔ Evaluation criteria used ✔ Effective individual work	✔ Evaluation criteria applied consistently ✔ Effective individual contribution to group	✔ Evaluation criteria defined and applied consistently ✔ Effective collaboration in a group of 5

Chapter One

Get thinking: get learning!

- Brain gain   8
- Learner's recipe   10
- Most wanted (1)   12
- Most wanted (2)   14
- Don't worry; be happy!   16
- Le Fevre Plus teaching board   18
- Apollo thinking   20

It is advisable to start with this chapter as it covers fundamental skills which children can then apply to tasks within specific subject areas.

The chapter begins with **Brain gain,** which requires children to work together to design a creative brain for a 'Holo Human'.

In **Learner's recipe,** children create a recipe for a competition. However, this is a recipe for the best learner, rather than a meal. Children must consider the qualities and skills that result in effective learning.

Most wanted (1) requires each child to create a poster about themselves – about their physical appearance and personal qualities. We often find it difficult to express the things that we do well but referring to

Gardner's Multiple Intelligences theory helps us to think about these things. The children complete an MI questionnaire and transfer the results to their 'most wanted' poster.

Most wanted (2) follows on from this: children create successful teams by looking at the skills and qualities that individuals in the class possess.

In **Don't worry; be happy!** children explore different emotions by creating a new character in Blob Land. (A Blob can only experience one emotion.) This activity helps children to develop emotional intelligence – the skills to recognise, name and express their various feelings in appropriate and effective ways. The children in your class will have a range of emotional sensitivity: autistic children, for example, may need specific help. For some of these children this activity might help them begin to understand the mechanics of emotions, even if they are not able to experience them subjectively.

The **Le Fevre Plus teaching board** activity offers guidance on how to monitor children's thinking and learning progress using Jonathan Le Fevre's method of learner mapping.

Apollo thinking develops children's problem-solving skills. Referring to the Apollo space mission for inspiration, children are encouraged to solve problems using limited resources and time.

Brain gain

Setting the context

It's 3010 and humankind has evolved beyond all recognition. Humans are now New-Humans. They have electronically programmed joints, bullet-proof skin, computerised muscles and brains filled with nano-machines that speed up thoughts, increase memory and enhance logical thinking. Some humans even opt for expensive upgrades that improve these skills further. These are the super-logical New+ Humans. Everyone wants to be a New+ Human. Everyone that is, except the Holo Humans. They are not happy with all these level-headed enhancements. They think it is boring and insist on being upgraded with wacky, creative brain extras instead. Certain backstreet scientists will upgrade a brain with enriched creativity but it is illegal! The most infamous clinic is run by Dr Rebecca Neuron. In Rebecca's lab, a Holo Human can have a new wacky brain fitted. But it's a dangerous business…

The challenge

Dr Neuron needs to persuade the Holo Humans to visit her for a brain upgrade. Help her to create a new super brain, the Holo Brain 3000. It must be imaginative, weird, fun and creative.

Objectives

To develop decision-making skills: making choices about materials and resources that best represent an idea.
To work creatively and collaboratively to strict time limits and with limited resources.
To explore how the brain is used for original thinking, creativity, imagination and emotions as well as logical thinking.

You will need

Copies of Dr Neuron's advert for her new Holo brain from photocopiable page 22, alternatively create one enlarged version to show to the whole class; drawing materials; coloured A5 card; safe access to scissors; a variety of materials such as junk modelling material, paint, sequins, feathers, buttons, coloured pipe cleaners, balloons, colour supplements; glue and sticky tape. You will also need a visible way to count down 50 minutes such as a classroom clock, a sand timer or LDA's 'Time Timer'.

Preparation

If you choose to role play Dr Neuron for the lesson you will need to prepare your costume, for example, a futuristic-type lab coat with wires poking out of a pocket. You could even wear dark glasses or ski/welding goggles. Gather together the tools and materials for the children and place them in plastic dishes or in a central resource area. You might like to prepare a 'Holo Brain 3000' as an example for the children. Prepare a 'Levels of success' chart to display on a whiteboard or flipchart, incorporating the success criteria outlined in the 'What to do' section. The success of the Holo brain will depend on how many criteria each child includes in his/her design.

What to do

● Explain the context and problem to the children and show them photocopiable page 22.
● Tell the children that they will have 50 minutes to make a brain for Dr Neuron.
● Ask them what their Holo Brain 3000 has to include, referring back to the advert. Invite them to ask questions about the advert and then make sure that you all agree on the following success criteria for building a Holo Brain 3000. It must:

1. Be about the same size as an adult head.
2. Show the paths of thought waves.
3. Have an area for creativity.
4. Have an area for emotion.
5. Have an area for imagination.
6. Have an area for generating weird and wacky thoughts.
7. Have an area for generating fun.
8. Have a socket to connect to the outside world.

● Organise the children into pairs or groups of three or let them choose one or two other children to work with.

● Tell the children to discuss with their partner(s) what they have been asked to do and give them an opportunity to clarify their understanding with you.

● Remind them that they will have only 50 minutes to build the brain.

● Show them the available tools and resources.

Drawing together

● After exactly 50 minutes, ask the children to place their brain (finished or not) in a designated display area.

● Ask the learners to look at their finished brains and assess how well they have met the criteria that were set.

● Demonstrate using the chart that you drew up at the preparation stage, then let the children use this chart to assess each others' brains (it is acceptable for a brain to meet criteria from different columns).

● Encourage the children to ask questions about each others' brains.

Support

● Carefully arrange the class into appropriate groups.

● Extend or reduce the time allowed.

● Suggest starting points and materials to use, for example, base the brain on an egg box and ask children to dedicate each section of the box to a different aspect of the brain.

● Adapt the success criteria to ensure that children are stretched but able to achieve success.

Extension

● Reduce the time allowed to make children think more quickly or extend the time allowed and expect a more developed, original brain.

● Encourage children to find more information about how the brain is creative and/or imaginative and how it handles emotions. Then ask them to make suggestions for adapting their Holo Brain 3000s.

Learner's recipe

(inspired by an idea from Steve Bowkett)

Setting the context

Madame Soufflé, the well-known TV chef, is famous for her original recipes and tasty, nutritious meals. She is a genius when it comes to combining unusual ingredients into delicious meals. Many top chefs go to her for advice but, strangely, different people have now started asking her for guidance. You see, recipes are not just for the world of cooking. A recipe is a special set of instructions to help you make something and you could use one in an office, a shop or a school just as easily. Your headteacher has written to Madame Soufflé asking for help. She and your headteacher have set up a competition challenging you to write a recipe for making the best learner. Instead of food, the ingredients will be skills and qualities – the things that go together to produce an effective and happy learner.

The challenge

Create a recipe for a successful learner to enter into Madame Soufflé's competition?

Objectives

To identify at least six different learning skills and six learning qualities.

To discover that a successful learner needs a wide and effective mix of skills and personal qualities.

To develop collaboration skills within a large group (class).

To learn how to apply a recipe format in a non-food context.

You will need

Three pieces of lining paper or similar, each 2–3 metres in length, to make three writing walls; a felt-tipped pen for each learner; copies of the recipe writing frame from photocopiable page 23; some sample recipes – one copy per pair.

Preparation

Fix each of the three pieces of lining paper (or similar) across the walls of the classroom, at a height where the children can easily write on each piece. Write the following titles on the paper, one title on each piece: 'Recipe Quantities'; 'Recipe Actions'; 'Learning Skills and Learning Qualities'. Prepare a 'Levels for success' chart to display on a whiteboard or flipchart: see opposite. Enlarge a copy of the recipe writing frame to show the class (see page 23). You may also want to dress up as Madame Soufflé at the end of the activity, or at a later date, to judge the competition.

What to do

● Share the scenario with the children.

● Distribute the recipe examples and ask the children to identify the key features of a recipe.

● Show them a large copy of the effective learner's recipe writing frame.

● Stand by each of the three 'writing walls' and, at each one in turn, add a few examples. Ask a couple of the children for their ideas and allow them to demonstrate writing their own ideas on the walls. (The ideas that your children produce will provide a benchmark indicating how aware they are of this aspect of learning. They may need a lot of input from you at this point. If so, here are a few skills and qualities to get them started: thinking, love of reading, cooperation.)

● Give each child a felt-tipped pen and give the class 10 minutes in which to silently visit each of the three writing walls, adding ideas and reading each others' contributions.

● After 10 minutes or when all their ideas have been added, ask the children to choose some ideas from the writing walls and use these to create their own recipe for an effective learner. Give them a few examples of how to do this:

● Add a pint of determination and a knob of curiosity together in a bowl.
Sieve in 100g of good thinking and beat together until it forms a sticky dough.

● Ask them to complete their learner's recipe writing frame.

Drawing together

● When the recipes are complete, bring the children together and ask them to share their work and learning.

● Ask individuals or pairs to read each others' recipes, looking specifically for similarities and differences.

● Establish the skills and qualities that keep being mentioned and take a note of these. They could, at a later date, be used to create a whole-class effective learner recipe.

● Ask the children to assess each others' recipes using the success criteria from the chart below.

© 2008 JupiterImages Corporation

Support

● Allow children to use the writing frame and adapt it if necessary.

● Let children work in pairs.

● Extend the time allowed and provide adult support.

● Allow children to record the recipe on a tape recorder rather than on paper.

Extension

● Invite children to create their own unique recipe format based on a recipe book layout. They could also create a recipe for an effective teacher or apply the recipe creation method to a school, a playtime or a local community.

Levels of success

Not there yet ☆	Nearly there ☆☆	Fantastic ☆☆☆
✔ Less than three criteria met	✔ At least three criteria met	✔ All criteria met
✔ Worked alone	✔ Worked with others for some of the time	✔ Worked successfully with others: shared roles
✔ Not finished yet	✔ Not quite finished, or finished after 30 minutes	✔ Finished in 45–50 minutes

Most wanted (1)

Setting the context

When someone has been a particularly successful criminal, they get to be very famous. Their picture appears on television, in newspapers and on street corners. They get to star in their very own 'most wanted' publicity campaign. A 'most wanted' poster could include a picture of the criminal, a description of what they look like and sound like, and, most importantly, an account of what they have done. It is a very effective way of telling a lot of people about one person with the aim of catching them and putting them in prison. However, 'most wanted' posters have another use. Sometimes they can be used to find good things or things that have been lost. We're going to make 'most wanted' posters for ourselves and tell everyone about our best features.

The challenge

Design and produce a 'most wanted' poster about yourself that includes a physical description or picture of you with a list of your best skills, qualities and achievements. Your poster will be part of a class display.

Objectives

To know at least eight personal skills or qualities.
To be able to create a personal profile in a 'most wanted' format.
To learn to design and create independently.

You will need

Copies of the questionnaire from photocopiable page 24 and the poster template from photocopiable page 25, for each learner.

Preparation

Prepare a 'most wanted' poster for yourself and, if you have time, find a couple of examples of 'most wanted' posters – for example real or fictional characters from the Wild West or present-day photo-fit images and their accompanying descriptions (make sure that the crime committed is suitable to share with your class).

What to do

● Be aware that some children in your class may have relatives in prison. Alter this task to a small-ads scenario if necessary.
● Share a 'most wanted' poster with the

MOST WANTED!

Qualities
Always cheerful and friendly

Best skills
Writing stories, painting and playing the violin

Achievements
Football captain

Year 5
School Council representative

Sheriff's badge © 2008 JupiterImages Corporation

children and ask them to identify the key features an image and a name; a description of the person; an account of what they have done.

● Explain that the purpose of a 'most wanted' poster is to find the person who has committed the crime.

● Share your own 'most wanted' poster with the children, making sure to explain to them that you are not a criminal.

● Show how you have chosen your 'most wanted' positive features.

● Ask the children to work individually and to fill out their own 'most wanted' questionnaires (photocopiable page 24).

● When these are complete, ask the children to use the results to complete their very own 'most wanted' posters (some children may wish to use the template provided on photocopiable page 25).

● Advise the children to choose their best feature to go in the heading on the poster, for example: 'Wanted For: Good Listening'.

Drawing together

● As the children complete their posters, pin them up in a designated area of the classroom, maybe naming the display 'Rogues' Gallery' or 'Hall of Fame'.

● Ask the children to look at each others' posters and look for features that some children have in common with each other.

● Challenge them to:

1. Find someone whose features nearly match theirs.

2. Find someone who is completely different to them.

3. Look carefully to see if the image on a poster is like the real person.

4. Consider what a particular person would contribute to a group in which they were working.

Support

● Request that all children use the 'most wanted' template.

● Reduce the number of features required in the poster, or allow other features to be included that do not appear on the questionnaire.

Extension

● Cover up the names on the completed posters and challenge children to match the poster descriptions to their classmates.

● Ask children to create a 'most wanted' poster for someone else, such as another pupil from another class, another teacher or a family member. Create a 'most wanted' poster for a group or team (see page 25).

● Ask the children to write a description of themselves when learning that includes some of their skills and qualities.

Most wanted (2)

Setting the context

Wow! What a talented bunch we are! I wonder what would happen if we put our skills together and worked in teams? Do you realise just how effective a team can be? If I give you a task to do on your own and 20 minutes to do it in, you might have the right skills or you might not. But what if you are in a team of five and I give you 20 minutes? Suddenly, you've got five times as many skills. Tasks can be split into smaller parts with each group member being responsible for something that uses their skills. How good is that?!

When you get your first job, your boss might want you to work in a team, perhaps with people you don't like that much, but you'll still have to do it. When we learn and work together we can achieve far more than we could alone.

The challenge

Look carefully at the 'most wanted' posters and combine them into groups of five or six people who you think would work and learn effectively together.

Objectives

To know that a successful team needs a range of skills and qualities to collaborate effectively.
To learn how to fulfil a role within a group and use individual strengths.
To discuss, debate and reach an agreement with others.

You will need

All of the 'most wanted' posters displayed in a way that all of the children can have easy access to them. You can do this in two ways:
Option 1: Create a reduced-size set of 'most wanted' posters from the previous activity. If the posters are A4, photocopy them in pairs (A3 together) reducing the pairs down to A4, giving two A5-sized posters. Then, if quality allows, photocopy-reduce two of these down onto A4. You'll then have four posters reduced onto A4 (4 x A6 posters). Cut up and make several packs of profiles (one pack per five children in the class).
Option 2: Photocopy the A4 posters and set up two identical galleries in different parts of the classroom. Half of the class can look at one gallery, half at the other gallery.

Preparation

Provide access to the 'most wanted' posters. Have in mind the essential qualities that you would want in your learning groups and consider possible effective groupings. Be ready to tweak and adjust the children's choices to help create effective groups. Prepare a 'Levels of success' chart on a whiteboard or flipchart (see opposite).

What to do

● Recap the tasks undertaken in the first 'most wanted' activity and share the context above with your class.

● Ask the children to form friendship groups of between four and six people.

● Issue the following task:

1. In your group, look at all the 'most wanted' profiles (either the mini-packs or in a gallery).

2. Based on the qualities and features shown by the class, which ones are needed for an effective group? Make a list.

● Make sure that the children understand that this activity is about true collaboration and not friendship groupings: they should think about what an effective group needs and who will be able to contribute these skills and qualities.

● Bring friendship groups back together and agree on the essentials that a group must have (have a 'wish list' and be mentally ticking it off – add your own ideas if the children omit them).

● Ask friendship groups to plan the organisation of the class into groups of five or six where all the essential skills and qualities are represented. Ask them to record their choices.

● Discuss the success criteria below, or create your own.

● To help the children focus, tell them that this is not about friendship groups, it is about combining the necessary skills for effective group work. Suggest a typical group task to help them focus: ask them to imagine that the groups they are forming will have to make a poster and do a presentation.

Drawing together

● Ask the groups of children in turn to present their decisions.

● Check that each group has met the success criteria discussed, or created, during the lesson.

● Choose what you believe to be the most workable solution and suggest that those groups try working together in another creative activity in the future and see what happens.

Support

● Allow children to work in friendship groups.

● Alter the group size and adult input to suit the needs of the class.

● Limit the number of profiles that children have to choose from or pre-select a small number of profiles that include a range of skills and qualities.

Extension

● Ask children to create specialist groups for specific tasks, for example, a science group, an art team, a group to make a model or a radio show. They should consider the specific skills/ qualities needed for unique jobs.

● Suggest person-swaps between two groups that will benefit both groups.

Levels of success

Not there yet ☆	Nearly there ☆☆	Fantastic ☆☆☆
✔ Less than half of the 'essential' criteria met	✔ At least half the 'essential' criteria met	✔ All 'essential' criteria met
✔ Did not listen to each other	✔ Listened to each other some of the time	✔ Listened to each other all of the time
✔ Chose friends only.	✔ Chose some group members based on skills	✔ Chose all group members based on skills

Don't worry; be happy!

Setting the context

Blob people live in Blob Land and they have very simple lives. Each Blob person feels one, and only one, emotion all the time and is called by that emotion. In Blob Land you'll meet Blob Surprise, Blob Disgusted, Blob Sad, Blob Angry, Blob Happy and Blob Frightened. All Blob people have the same goal in life, to make other Blob people feel their particular emotion. So, for example, Blob Happy might devote a whole day to cheering up Blob Sad, while Blob Sad will do all he can to take the wind out of Blob Happy's sails. But Blob Land is becoming boring! The same six emotions keep getting passed around.

The Blob people have decided to work together to create some more Blob people with new emotions. They are going to do this by blending together – a process called swumpling – where two or more Blob people donate a little piece of themselves, mix it up and make a completely new Blob person with a brand new emotion.

The challenge

Create a new Blob person to liven things up in Blob Land.

Objectives

To understand and be aware of a wide range of emotions.
To consider how different emotions affect learning.
To explore how to create a 3D representation of an emotion.

You will need

Lots of Plasticine®, play dough or similar in six distinct colours; a list of emotions from photocopiable page 26 (for display, or one for each pair).

Preparation

Consolidate your own knowledge and understanding of emotions and consider your responsibilities in class as a role model of emotional intelligence. Experiment with the combination of basic emotions to make more complicated ones. For example, fear combined with anger could be jealousy; happiness and fear could result in nervousness; happiness and surprise could make amazement. Experiment with your modelling materials and make a couple of Blob people. Give them features to match their emotions, for example, wide eyes, high eyebrows and arms in the air for surprise.

What to do

● Read out the context to the children.
● Show the children a Blob person that you made earlier and ask them to discuss with a partner what the name of your Blob person might be and why.
● Explain how you shaped the material to express emotion (for example a Blob stooped over with a down-turned mouth would be Blob Sad).
● Introduce the modelling material to the children and set ground rules for its use.
● Ask individuals or pairs to quickly (in 5 minutes) create one of the six Blob people

Backdrop and models by Linda Jones
Photograph 2008 Scholastic Ltd

using the following success criteria (make sure several of each Blob person are made – not all Blob Happys). Each Blob person should: be between 5 and 10cm tall; have head, arms and legs (how many is not stated!); have a face or other features to express emotion; be one colour (each emotion should be represented by a different colour).

● Stop the children and share the list of possible new emotions (hand out copies of photocopiable page 26 or display one enlarged copy).

● Ask them to get together with two or three other people and 'swumple' – create a new Blob person by tearing off and combining parts of two or three existing Blob people. Tell the children to secretly select an emotion from the list, discuss quietly how to get the new Blob person to show this emotion, and then make it.

● The original Blob people can be reformed using the remaining material (only smaller).

Drawing together
● Display the new Blob people.
● Tell the children to look at each others' work and try to guess which emotion each Blob person is (from the list). Invite the children to write their guesses on Post-It Notes® and stick them next to each model.
● Ask each group to reveal the emotion they were attempting to express.

Support
● Demonstrate facial features and body postures that express different emotions.
● Concentrate on creating the original Blob people – avoid swumpling!
● Provide images of people showing different emotions.
● Use 'Emotional Matchcards' from educational resources suppliers TTS or similar.

Extension
● Take digital photos of a selection of Blob people and then build them into a PowerPoint® show about Blob Land or a photo story from Blob Land.
● Create a conversation between two or more Blob people.
● Animate Blob people (PowerPoint® slides on very fast automatic transition).
● Create a play about Blob Land and perform it to fellow pupils, teachers and parents.

Page
17

Le Fevre Plus teaching board
(a creative activity for you!)

Setting the context

The creative activities in this book are intended to be spread over several terms. For example, you might choose to make every Wednesday afternoon or every other Friday morning 'creative time'. Over the months, your children will experience, develop and consolidate a wide range of skills which can be applied outside of 'creative time'. It is important to develop continuity between activities (especially if they are separated by several days or weeks). It is also wise to show the children just how well they are progressing in the development of their thinking and learning skills. A Le Fevre Plus teaching board is an excellent way to address these points. The concept was invented by Jonathan Le Fevre, a headteacher working in Hampshire, and develops further the idea as introduced in *Creative Activities: Thinking and Learning Skills 5–7*.

The challenge

How can we develop continuity and show progression of the thinking and learning skills that are being developed through these creative activities?

Objectives

To be able to show the development and progression of the full range of thinking and learning skills on a Le Fevre board.
To explore how the board can be used to show how one activity might link to the previous one as well as the next.
To be involved in the use and development of the board.

You will need

A small display space near to the lesson delivery area; access to clipart or other images; a digital camera; a PC; a printer; display-making materials and equipment; Velcro® and card.

Preparation

On a display wall near to your lesson delivery area, create a mind-map style display which includes a central image to represent thinking and learning skills, for example, a brain and a hand; a central title such as the words, 'Learning to learn; learning to think'; eight areas around the central image, each with a suitable image:

    Creative thinking
    Using thinking
    Managing thoughts
    Thinking about thinking
    Collaborative learning
    Independent learning
    Learning about learning
    Knowing how I learn

Attach a piece of Velcro® next to the image for each area; make six gold card ticks or stars and fix the opposite Velcro® on the back of each one so they can be attached to the display when needed.

What to do

● Your Le Fevre board is multi-purpose and can be adapted to different teaching and learning styles. Here are several ways to use it to address progression and continuity:

● At the beginning of a creative (or other) learning activity, after sharing the context: ask the children which skills they will be developing and stick a star or tick next to each one on the board; ask the children which skills they worked on last time and whether there were any targets for improvement.

● During the activity: observe evidence of the skills in action, write your observations on Post-It Notes® and fix the notes to the board; take digital photos of the skills in action.

● At the end of an activity: refer back to the board and the stars or ticks and ask the children which skills they used and how well they used them; ask the children to set targets for improvement based on the skills; agree on additional words and images to add to the board. For example, it might be suggested that one aspect of 'Managing thoughts' is 'sorting' in which case the word 'sorting' and an image of a drawer of socks could be added.

● Before the next activity: print out photos that clearly show the skills in action and stick them to the appropriate part of the Le Fevre Plus board; make laminated name tags for each child and invite them to stick their name next to their best skill; take a digital photo of the board as a record of the children's self-assessment; ask children to nominate each other for using a skill well and place the nominee's name on the board. Again take a photo.

● Take a photo of the blank display, print it onto A4 card (one copy for each child), laminate it and use it as a learning mat (see page 28, 'The magic writing mat', for learning mat details).

Drawing together

● Make continual reference to the board and its evolution throughout the year.

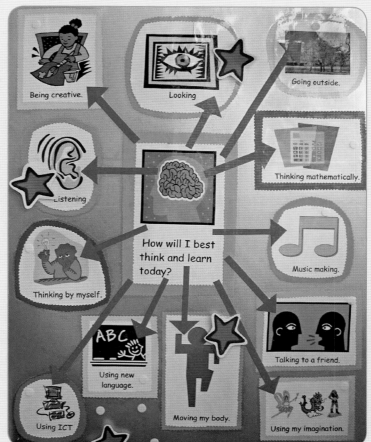

Being creative. Looking. Going outside. Listening. Thinking mathematically. How will I best think and learn today? Thinking by myself. Music making. Using new language. Moving my body. Talking to a friend. Using ICT. Using my imagination.

Photograph © Lynne Williams

● Allow the children to suggest how it might develop and be used in different ways.

● Make it explicit to the children that the board is there to help them realise how the creative activities connect together; and to show how everyone is improving their thinking and learning skills.

Support

● Value each child for their existing skill strengths.

● Give many real, concrete examples of what a skill is and what it looks like.

Extension

● Focus on the 'meta' areas, i.e. Thinking about thinking; Learning about learning.

● Allow the children to apply the Le Fevre Plus concept to create their own boards. These could be subject-specific or related to a career or profession or linked to a hobby or leisure pursuit.

Apollo thinking

Setting the context

The crew members of the Apollo 13 mission were saved by the creativity of a group of scientists and engineers on Earth. Under time pressure, they laid out only the materials and equipment available to the astronauts in Apollo 13. They worked with these limited resources to produce a life-saving solution to the problem of a damaged space craft. Let's copy this scientific way of problem solving. In teams you'll get limited resources and time to come up with a solution to one of the following problems:

1. A thief is stealing ice-creams, buckets and spades from children on the beach.
2. The show starts in 15 minutes, the orchestra has arrived but the instruments have not.
3. A blind scientist needs to be able to find his way around the laboratory.
4. Rats are overrunning our public buildings.

The challenge

Solve one of the problems above within a set time and with limited resources.

Objectives

To learn to solve problems with limited resources and under strict time pressure.
To develop creative thinking skills, using objects in ingenious ways.
To improve listening skills.

You will need

A visible timing method; a short film clip of the Apollo 13 mission (optional); ten random objects with which to solve the problems such as: a wine glass, a £10 note, a calculator, five metres of string, some silly string, a box of matches, a tape recorder, a tennis ball, a newspaper, a torch.

Preparation

Assemble the random materials for demonstration only. Think up some problems in addition to the ones suggested. Research the Apollo 13 mission and either have an account of the mission to hand or locate a suitable film clip to show the children.

What to do

● If possible, show a short film clip of Apollo 13 and recount the Apollo 13 story to the children. (Two days after launching, the spacecraft was damaged by an explosion caused by a fault in the oxygen tank. This resulted in a loss of oxygen and electrical power. The crew used the lander portion of the spacecraft as a 'lifeboat'. The main systems remained functional, but were deactivated to preserve the vehicle's ability to re-enter Earth's atmosphere. Despite having little power, cabin heat or water, the crew successfully returned to Earth.)

● Describe the problem-solving strategy that the children will be using: they will have limited time and limited random resources.

● Organise the children into groups of four and allow them to choose one person from their group to write down the ten items available to solve the problem.

● Give all groups the same problem to solve (see 'Context') and five minutes to come up

with a creative solution using only the ten items available.

● Call them back together and ask them to share their ideas.

● Ask them if any additional items would have helped.

● Offer three further problems and allow groups to choose which one they tackle.

● Set another five minutes, but this time ask for at least two different solutions.

Drawing together

● Draw the children together and invite each group to talk about the new problem they tackled and the solutions they came up with.

● Encourage them to evaluate their group work by asking the following questions: *What strategies did you develop? How well did your group work when it was under pressure? Were there any problems in the group? Do you work better under time pressure? Does everyone?*

Support

● Allow children more time.

● Suggest simple problems and more obvious objects to stimulate their solutions. (For example, the problem is a cat stuck up a tree and the resources available to solve the problem are lots of wood, nails and a saw.)

Extension

● Apply this problem-solving strategy directly to other curriculum areas.

● Reduce the number of objects available, encouraging children to think more creatively about the objects they do have.

● Ask children to set their own problems and challenge each other to solve them.

Brain gain

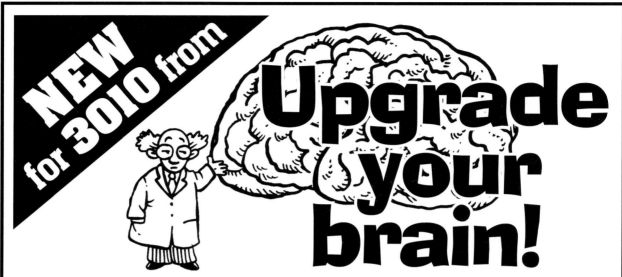

NEW for 3010 from

Upgrade your brain!

Dr Rebecca Neuron presents:

Holo Brain 3000

- Painless retro-fit to existing human skull
- Untraceable thought waves
- Creativity engine mark 7.3
- Emotion processing module
- Imagination hub
- Weird and wacky injection protocol
- Fun infusion program
- Docking port for easy wetware upgrades
- Unique configuration – no two brains the same

For a free consultation and to book a brain viewing:
Head-Text: Brains 784651
Mind Mail: Rebecca@bru.fiz

Learner's recipe

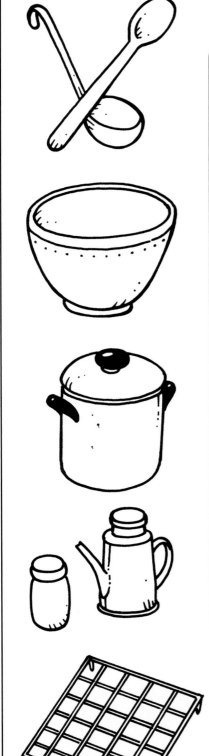

Recipe for an effective learner

You will need:

Skills:

1 _____

2 _____

3 _____

4 _____

5 _____

6 _____

Qualities:

1 _____

2 _____

3 _____

4 _____

5 _____

6 _____

Directions:

1 _____

2 _____

3 _____

4 _____

5 _____

6 _____

7 _____

Illustration © 2008 Moreno Chiacchiera

Most wanted (1)
questionnaire

	I can read well			I am good at working out how other people feel
	I can listen well			I can cheer people up
	I can talk my way out of trouble			I know who to ask if I have a problem
	I can persuade people to do things			I love learning
	I have a great imagination			I love animals
	I can do maths easily			I love being outside
	I can write well			I enjoy my own company
	I am good at board games like chess			I know what I am good at
	I'm good at making plans			I know what I want to do in the future
	I can ask good questions			When I have a problem, I can sort it out myself
	I am really creative			
	I enjoy doing jigsaw puzzles			I have the respect of other people
	I am good at following maps			I can name lots of plants/animals
	I am good at art			Other people trust me
	I can take calculated risks			Other people ask me for advice
	I am good at sport			I am a deep thinker
	I am good at building things			I care for the world
	I am good at fixing things			I can meditate
	I can lead a team well			I am interested in new ideas
	I have got a good sense of humour			I pray now and again
	I am good at singing			I often think about life, the universe and everything
	I can remember tunes and songs easily			
	I know a lot about music			
	I am very organised			
	I can work and learn on my own			

Most wanted (1)

WANTED

For:

Name: _____

HEAD PROFILE

HEAD FACE ON

Description:

- _____
- _____
- _____
- _____
- _____
- _____
- _____

Features:

- _____
- _____
- _____
- _____
- _____
- _____
- _____

Features keen to develop:

- _____
- _____
- _____
- _____
- _____
- _____

Don't worry; be happy!

● Choose one emotion from the list below and create a new Blob person.

amazement

despair

loneliness

guilt

hatred

nervousness

curiosity

impatience

jealously

enthusiasm

respect

relief

joy

Illustration © 2008 Moreno Chiacchiera

■SCHOLASTIC
www.scholastic.co.uk

Chapter Two

Thinking, learning and literacy

- The magic writing mat   28
- Multi-metaphor me   30
- Dear Sir/Madam   32
- MI library   34
- Fairy tale jigsaw   36
- Distant voices   38

This chapter helps children to develop the thinking and learning skills introduced in chapter one within the context of literacy.

- The chapter begins with **The magic writing mat** in which children create a writing mat for the mayor of Greyville to help him write an exciting story. This introduces the idea of a learning mat: an A4 or A3 laminated card on which there is a simple and colourful summary of a topic or subject area (such as imaginative writing).

- **Multi-metaphor me** can be used to introduce or revise what a metaphor is. In this activity the children create metaphors to describe themselves.

- **Dear Sir/Madam…** encourages children to think creatively about everyday objects, in this case, the drawing pin. They explore how to improve its design, showing them that even the simplest things are open to innovation. When children are asked to be creative, some find it daunting, especially if their strengths lie in spheres other than original thinking. Yet creative thinking is easy when you provide simple starting points. Many of the ideas played around with in an activity like this will be interesting but useless. However, one or two might be that gem of an idea that makes all the difference!

- In **MI library** children plan a reorganisation of the school library around the nine areas of Multiple Intelligences. This activity requires children to collaborate with each other and develop an awareness of different learning styles.

- **Fairy tale jigsaw** encourages children to think creatively about traditional fairy tales. They combine elements of different tales to create their own original stories.

- The final activity in this chapter, **Distant voices**, is based around a short animated film by Makoto Shinkai, which explores communication. Children write text messages to a range of people in different situations, distilling their ideas into brief communications, while maintaining appropriate meaning and purpose.

The magic writing mat

Setting the context

Everything in Greyville is boring. The people have dreary eyes, set mouths and they shuffle about all day between their boring homes and boring jobs. The citizens of Greyville mumble to each other over their weak tea and meals of bread, bread and more bread! There's only one programme on TV. It's called, 'How to keep breathing in two easy steps' and only one book has ever been published, 'How to use the word "Then" as often as possible' by Greyville's only author, Mr A Dull. The people of Greyville are becoming so bored that they are fading away. Already this year, 10 per cent of the population has just stopped bothering to exist. The mayor is a little bit concerned, when he can be bothered, and feels he should do something about it. Maybe a new TV show or another book would help. Maybe he should write a story with a bit of... what was the word?... ex-cite-ment!

The challenge

Create a magic writing mat for the mayor to help him put the excitement back into Greyville.

Objectives

To develop collaboration skills.
To explore how to create imaginative solutions to problems.
To learn how to make writing more interesting and engaging.
To develop sorting skills so that information is easily communicated.

You will need

Examples of interesting, engaging, exciting writing – from established authors and the children themselves; A4 and A3 paper and card; coloured pencils and pens; access to images – clipart, colour supplements and so on; a colour scanner and printer; an A4/A3 laminator and laminating sleeves.

Preparation

Ensure that you and the children are familiar with the concept of a learning mat. A learning mat is a classroom tool that can be used in many different ways. It is often an A4 or A3 laminated card on which there is a simple and colourful summary of a topic or subject area. You could have a learning mat on the Romans, times tables, tricky spellings or classroom rules. The mat's purpose is to act as an individual, interactive reminder of key points. Children can use whiteboard pens to write on comments and responses and, as the mat is laminated, these can also be wiped off. For example, a learning mat called 'How to write an interesting sentence' could include definitions, examples, word banks, ideas and reference suggestions. Children could circle the words they will use to enrich their writing. For this activity, define the content that you want your learners to include on their magic writing mats: the features you hope to see in their own writing. For example: a range of types of sentences, exciting adjectives, a range of connectives, interesting metaphors. Be guided by the writing curriculum which your school follows. Finally, on a flipchart or whiteboard,

draw up a 'Levels of success' chart showing the criteria for the children to refer to when assessing their work at the end of the activity.

What to do

● Share the context of Greyville with the children.
● Share a piece of exciting writing with them and draw their attention to the key features that make it exciting.
● Make a list of the features which the children identify and add the ones they miss.
● Develop with the children a rough visual plan for a magic writing mat (see success criteria below).
● Organise the children into groups of four or five and ask them to allocate the following roles:
    1. Writing expert (someone who knows about excellent writing).
    2. Facilitator (someone who is skilled at managing groups).
    3. Artist (someone who is skilled at expressing ideas in images).
    4. Timekeeper (someone who has a good sense of time and can keep everyone focused on the task).
    5. Checker (someone who is good at making sure everything has been done as asked).
All of the children should contribute ideas alongside their individual roles.
● Ask the groups to design and create a magic writing mat to the following success criteria: the mat should include lots of examples and ideas; it should incorporate at least three different colours and at least four images; it should completely cover an A4 or A3 sheet; it should have correct spelling, grammar and punctuation and clear, legible writing.
● Tell the children that during the activity you will be observing them to make sure that everyone in the group contributes to the task.

Drawing together

Ask groups to assess each others' mats against the success criteria. How many met all of the criteria? Did all group members work hard? What more could you have achieved if you had another five minutes?
● Colour-scan, print and laminate mats ready to use in future class writing tasks.
● To round off the activity, ask each group to assess its own product and collaboration using the 'Levels of success' chart that you prepared earlier.

Support
● Place children in a group where their strengths are valued and their weaknesses are supported.
● Provide a learning mat template – see photocopiable page 40.

Extension
● Create magic mats for other purposes, for example: solving maths problems, keeping the classroom tidy, making and keeping friends, playground behaviour.
● Refer to the mats when writing.
● Assess own and others' writing by marking on the mat with a whiteboard pen.
● Use a large version of the mat, either printed out or on an interactive whiteboard, for whole-class assessment of writing.
● Give children individual paper copies of the mat to use for assessment and recording of writing progression. Mark them up at the end of each half-term.

Page
29

Multi-metaphor me

Setting the context

People often portray themselves to each other through a written or verbal description. This usually includes basic facts (eye colour, age and so on), history (where they live, major life events), family and job or school. These depictions can be rather dull and dry and don't really help you to understand what the person is really all about and what makes them tick. Metaphors can fix this. By describing yourself as something else with which you identify, you can genuinely express in an imaginative and interesting way who you are and what makes you unique: I am a sleek hound racing across the moor; I am a flute fading into the air; I am a church bell striking once.

The challenge

Use the Metaphor generator to creatively express the real you.

Objectives

To learn how to express personal qualities creatively using metaphors.
To develop independent and enterprise skills.
To learn to choose and then arrange ideas into a suitable format, such as a personal profile.

You will need

Copies of photocopiable page 41; access to a computer suite/laptop (optional); a metaphor template for less confident learners (see example on page 31)

Preparation

Use the Metaphor generator to create an imaginative description of yourself and be ready to share it with the children.

What to do

● Tell the children that you are going to describe yourself in two different ways. Firstly describe yourself using basic facts, then describe yourself using metaphors.
● Ask the children to discuss with a partner

how the two descriptions differed.
● Elicit from the children that a metaphor can add detail to a description and help it to become more useful, interesting and vivid.
● Discuss what the metaphors actually mean. For example, what does the phrase 'a flute fading into the air' suggest? (Perhaps something beautiful, but fragile and temporary.)
● Introduce the Metaphor generator and teach the children how to use it (see page 41) by creating a couple of metaphors for a chosen child.
● Ask pairs of children to create a metaphor

Nouns:
tree, skyscraper, bell, bird, scarecrow, wolf, cloud, mouse, lion, flower, mountain, iceberg

Verbs:
standing, running, skipping, lying, crying, laughing, ringing, sighing, singing, flying, hopping

Adjectives:
low, tall, cold, dark, spooky, sunny, warm, airy, stuffy, empty, friendly, lonely

Nouns (places):
room, forest, beach, castle, ocean, field

for each other.

● Listen to several of the children's metaphors and comment on their effectiveness at describing their partner.

● Set the children the task of creating an individual 'Multi-metaphor me' written description which includes the following success criteria:

1. It does not include your name.
2. It uses the starting points on the Metaphor generator.
3. It includes at least five different metaphors.

Drawing together

● Print and display the 'Multi-metaphor me' descriptions and challenge the children to match them to their classmates. Alternatively, ask the children to write their metaphors on some scrap paper and put them in a hat. As you pull out a name, ask the children to guess who wrote it.

● Ask the children to identify their favourite metaphors from all of those displayed.

Support

● Encourage children to create simple metaphors such as 'I am a fox', rather than 'I am a sly fox creeping through the trees'.

● Allow children to use a metaphor template (see example above). Give them four word groups and ask them to choose a word from each group.

Extension

● Create a 'Multi-metaphor' for a group, class, family or celebrity.

● Combine the best parts of several descriptions into a new one.

● Illustrate each metaphor with a simple line drawing or symbol.

● Create new metaphors from starting points other than those on the generator.

● Explore the difference between a metaphor and a simile.

Dear Sir/ Madam...

Setting the context

When things go wrong, one of the most civilised responses is to write a letter of complaint. If your order doesn't come on time or if something you've bought doesn't work, then writing a letter gets the anger off your chest and lets the guilty party know that something has gone wrong. If you're lucky, you'll get an apology, your money back or a replacement will be sent. If you're really lucky, you might get all three! Complaint letters usually follow a standard format.

But the complaint letter you're going to write needs a little extra sparkle and a great deal of creative skill. It's a letter of complaint to the world's largest supplier of drawing pins – Pins Ltd.

The challenge

Drawing pins are boring. Little brass things with a sharp point! Why can't they be fun and interesting like paper clips have become? Write a letter to Pins Ltd pointing out the problem and suggesting some creative possibilities.

Objectives

To learn how to use humour subtly and effectively.
To recognise and use prompts for creative thinking.
To know and use the key features of a letter of complaint.

You will need

Copies of photocopiable page 42 and copies of photocopiable page 43, enough for one per child.

Preparation

Visit: http://www.bbc.co.uk/consumer/how_to_complain/letters.shtml and http://www.businessballs.com complaintsletters.htm for information and examples of letters of complaint. Prepare a sample complaint letter for the children to read, or for you to read aloud to them. A genuine letter of your own will be far more interesting for them, especially if you have a tale to tell about the problem.

What to do

● Share your tale of woe and complaint letter with the children. If there is an interesting conclusion to the saga, let them know that you will reveal all at the end of the lesson.

● Read the scenario to the children. Discuss why it is important to question everyday objects such as the humble drawing pin or the glass window, and how this can easily be done. Start by choosing a feature of an object, then alter it in some way. Consider if and how the new object is better than the original. Here's an example: take the glass in a window, make it thicker. This gives you warmer rooms.

● Help the children understand that when several notional alterations are applied, then more innovative possibilities arise: make it bigger, smaller, a different colour, change the texture, material, add another one, remove half, combine it with something else, swap it and so on.

● Introduce the Creativity contraption from

page 43 and try it out by putting in a virtual bread roll. Discuss the effects of: making it bigger (will fill you up more, but might not fit in your lunch box); changing its colour (might make it more appealing, or make it stand out from all the other rolls, meaning you're more likely to buy it) and so on.
● Talk through the writing frame for a complaint letter on photocopiable page 42.
● Tell the children to complete the writing frame and use the Creativity contraption on page 43 to generate ideas for the 'Might I recommend that you...' section.

Drawing together
● Bring the children back together and role play the MD of Pins Ltd weeping while reading the children's letters, yet perking up at some of their more interesting ideas.
● Ask the children to suggest different uses for the generic complaint letter.
● Challenge the children to think of alternative uses for the Creativity contraption. Tell them to discuss their ideas with a partner and between them choose the best use for the contraption.
● If appropriate, tell the children the end/resolution of your personal complaint saga.

Support
● Ask children who are less confident at writing to draw or verbally describe the altered pins.
● Suggest which creative alterations to make to reduce the number of options.

Extension
● Ask children to apply the complaint letter template to other situations.
● Use the Creativity contraption to improve and develop other things such as story characters, towns, furniture, artwork, sports equipment and so on.
● Ask the children to suggest further alterations which the contraption could perform.

Page
33

MI library

Setting the context

We all have different skills and interests and we are all clever in our own ways. This means that we will succeed in different ways too. Some of us might be able to write songs and play instruments; others will be good at writing or maths; others at art or problem-solving. Everyone is good at something and everyone learns in a slightly different way. At the moment, the books in our school library are organised according to the Dewey Decimal System. Each book belongs to a category as well as a subject. As you work down the categories, the subjects get more specific, for example, 500 is Science, 590 Animals, 599 Mammals, 599.4 Bats. Now, Dr Tom Hoerr, the headteacher of a school in St Louis, USA, has created what is believed to be the world's first MI Library – a resource area for the whole school organised around the Multiple Intelligences.

The challenge

Plan a reorganisation of your school library around the nine areas of Multiple Intelligence. Suggest fiction and non-fiction texts as well as other learning resources that would go well in each area.

Objectives

To appreciate that everyone has a variety of valuable skills.
To recognise that everyone is intelligent and can become more so.
To develop collaboration skills.
To explore how to classify books and other learning resources.

You will need

Access to the school library; copies of photocopiable page 44, enough for one each or for children to share in groups of four to six.

Preparation

Children will need to have a working knowledge of MI theory and practice or at least an awareness of the nine different, yet equally valuable, areas of intelligence: music, words, deep thinking, nature, people, self, images, body, logic (often called 'Smarts'. They should also be familiar with the basic principles of the Dewey Decimal Classification™. (See www.oclc.org/dewey/resources/summaries/deweysummeries.pdf)

You may want to prepare a copy of the 'Levels of success' chart opposite for display on a whiteboard or flipchart.

What to do

● Take the children into the school library and together review its organisation around the Dewey Decimal Classification™.
● Point out the different top level categories:

    000 Generalities
    100 Philosophy & psychology
    200 Religion
    300 Social sciences
    400 Language
    500 Natural sciences & mathematics
    600 Technology (Applied sciences)
    700 The arts
    800 Literature & rhetoric
    900 Geography & history
and a few of the sub-categories.
● Remind the children of the nine areas of Multiple Intelligence and ask them to recall from previous activities where their own strengths lie. They could share their thoughts with the person next to them.

- Ask them to get into equal-sized groups with others who share a similar MI strength.
- Set all groups the following task, using the template on photocopiable page 44 to help organise the children's thoughts and ideas. Ask the children to plan a section of a new MI library for your school. Each group's plan must include at least ten examples of fiction; at least ten examples of non-fiction; at least five examples of learning tools or equipment (for example, body smarts might suggest bean bags and a sofa; logic smarts might suggest a computer and so on); a floor plan.
- Discuss the success criteria in the chart below and leave this on display for the children to refer to throughout the activity.
- Recommend to the children that they share out the tasks within the group and appoint a facilitator, a timekeeper and a plan drawer.

Drawing together
- When all the designs are finished, cut out the floor plans and arrange them into a display, asking children to add walls, doors and open areas to complete the new MI Library plan.
- Ask the children to evaluate their own designs and then each others' using the criteria below.
- Discuss whether they think an MI Library is better than one that uses the Dewey Decimal Classification™.

Support
Group children carefully and provide suggestions for each group as to what could go in their MI area to get them started.

Extension
- Apply the MI library process to your classroom.
- Suggest other possible library areas, for example, creativity, in the past, in the future, expensive, cheap.

Page

35

Levels of success

Not there yet ☆	Nearly there ☆☆	Fantastic ☆☆☆
✔ Plan only includes one or part: fiction, non-fiction, resources; wrong amounts	✔ Plan includes fiction, non-fiction books and learning resources, but wrong amounts	✔ Plan includes ten fiction and ten non-fiction books and five learning tools
✔ Plan not completed in the given time	✔ Plan almost completed in the given time	✔ Plan completed in the given time
✔ Didn't work well as a group	✔ Worked well in a group most of the time	✔ Worked well in a group: allocated roles

Fairy tale jigsaw

Setting the context

Once upon a time there was a man who knew the secret of how to write fairy tales. He was the only person who knew the secret. He wrote all the fairy stories that you've hopefully been hearing since the day you were born. But people had heard his tales so often that they had become tired of them. Little Red Riding Hood, The Three Little Pigs, Cinderella, Rumpelstiltskin and the rest – everyone knew them all, word for word, inside out and back to front. So they asked the man to make up some new stories. He started to play around with the characters and then he started to mess around with the places, the plots, the twists and the turns. He mixed them up and jumbled them about and when he had finished, he was rather pleased with himself because he had invented a whole new library of fairy tales.

The challenge

Use the ideas and characters in the fairy tales that you already know to create a brand new story in the same style to add to the new collection of fairy tales.

Objectives

To explore how existing ideas can be transformed into an original piece of writing. To develop a wide-ranging knowledge of the fairy tale genre.
To learn to write in the style of a fairy tale, selecting characters, plots and story motifs.

You will need

A selection of well-known fairy tales; copies of the jigsaw pieces from photocopiable page 45 and page 37, for each pair.

Preparation

Select a well-known fairy tale to retell to the children. Practise reading it aloud or telling it from memory.

What to do

● Read or retell a well-known fairy tale to the children

● Ask them to tell you about the main characters and the places in the story.

- Encourage them to also give you a simple plot summary.
- Ask the children, working in twos, to recall the titles of at least five fairy tales.
- List several fairy tales on a whiteboard or flipchart and discuss the key points of them: the main characters, the setting and the key elements of the plot.
- Point out any similarities: for example, most fairy tales have a hero or heroine who overcomes the evil intentions of a 'bad' character.
- Read out the context to the children and share with them the Fairy tale jigsaw on photocopiable page 45.
- Tell them to combine characters, plots and settings from different stories to stimulate ideas for a plan for an all-new fairy tale.
- Set limits such as:
  1. Choose no more than three characters.
  2. Choose two settings.
  3. Choose two plot features.
- Ask the children to write plans individually and then group the children into pairs to discuss their ideas with each other.
- You might want to take the ideas in at this point and continue the activity after you have assessed the children's ideas.
- Then, ask the children to write an original fairy tale from their plan.

Drawing together

- Select several children to read out their stories.
- While listening, tell the other children to note which characters, plots and settings have been used. They could write a list or tick them off on a copy of the jigsaw worksheet.
- Check that any limits set (see 'What to do') have been adhered to.
- Ask learners to read out their ideas to each other.

Extra piece of jigsaw for activity

Support
- Children could cut out ideas from the Fairy tale jigsaw.
- Those who are less confident at writing could plan and tell the story on tape/digital audio.
- Children could plan and write their stories in pairs if appropriate.

Extension
- Give each child a single jigsaw piece and ask them to get together with three others to see if they have a story in the making. Challenge them to create the story in three minutes and be ready to tell it to the class.
- Tell children that they should also include extra jigsaw pieces.
- Apply creativity to another genre of story: Greek myths; science fiction and so on.

Distant voices

Setting the context

Voices of a Distant Star is an animated film about love, separation, war and loss. For 30 minutes, it tells the story of teenagers Mikako and Noboru. Mikako joins an interstellar battle to help save Earth from alien invasion, while Noboru remains at home to study and lead his dull and lonely life. In the pain of being apart, their only method of communication is text messaging. At first, the signals take days to send; then weeks, months and finally years as Mikako is posted further and further away. She remains young as Noboru ages. The story makes you think about how fragile communication can be sometimes, and how careful we must be when choosing our words, especially if the message takes years to arrive.

The challenge

Write a series of very brief messages for a range of intriguing purposes and to a variety of people.

Objectives

To explore the purpose and power of written communication.

To consider the receiver of a communication and how they could misunderstand your words.

To learn to distil ideas down into their most important words.

You will need

A copy of the DVD, *Voices of a Distant Star* (Makoto Shinkai, Bones/Kurau Project, 2002, PG) and permission from parents for children to watch it; a copy of photocopiable page 46, for each child.

Preparation

Watch the DVD to familiarise yourself with the characters and plot so that you are able to talk knowledgeably about the film with the children. You may want to prepare a 'Levels of success' chart on a flipchart or whiteboard (see example opposite).

What to do

● Spend 30 minutes watching the film with the children and, as they watch, tell them to look out for the following: the text messages sent and the reactions of the boy and girl as they send, receive and anticipate messages.

● Ask the children to tell a partner about their observations.

● Ask them what text messages they would send to Mikako and Noboru.

● Introduce the communication ideas from photocopiable page 46 and ask the children to complete the first text message of sending a text to Mikako in space, working in pairs.

● Explain that communication by text message must fulfil the following requirements:

   1. Each text message must be less than ten words.

   2. It must be clear and it has to make sense.

   3. It is not always necessary to write in complete sentences.

   4. The language and content should be fit for purpose.

   5. Messages can be in text language but don't need to be.

● Display and discuss the criteria in the 'Levels of success' chart opposite.

● Listen to the children's ideas for their first text message.

● Tell them to choose and complete at least three further communications using ideas from the worksheet, explaining that the children can work alone or in pairs.

Maybe 2morrow you will come home.
I hope so.

Drawing together

● Ask the children to find someone else in the class who has chosen the same communication example from the worksheet. Have them compare the words that they used in their text messages.

● Arrange the whole class into groups of five or six and ask each group to swap text messages with another group. See if the children can guess who the message is intended for, from its content.

● Share some examples of text messages as a class and check each of them against the success criteria from the chart below.

● Draw attention to the 'text language' that the children may have used, for example, 'see you= c u'. As a 'teaser' for a possible follow on lesson, share a range of examples: http://en.wikipedia.org/wiki/SMS_language.

Support

● Provide more simple communication challenges, for example, to more familiar people in more concrete situations.

● Pair less confident learners with someone more confident in literacy.

Extension

● Tell children to develop two- or three-way conversations in text style. More confident learners could invent further communication scenarios and challenge each other to write text messages.

● View the DVD extras to gain a deeper insight into the story.

● Create graphic novel style images to illustrate scenes from the story.

Levels of success

Not there yet ☆	Nearly there ☆☆	Fantastic ☆☆☆
✔ Text is a lot over 10 words	✔ Text is a little over ten words	✔ Text is between 8 and 10 words
✔ It doesn't make sense	✔ It mostly makes sense	✔ It makes sense
✔ Language and content are not fit for purpose	✔ Language or content area not fit for purpose	✔ Language and content are both fit for purpose

The magic writing mat

then, so, next, eventually,

My favourite words:

Adjectives, nouns, verbs, adverbs:

Use lots of connectives

Pick up a dictionary/ thesaurus

DICTIONARY

Magic Writing Mat

Adjectives, nouns, verbs, adverbs

Use varied sentences

Discuss your ideas with another writer

A simple sentence =

A compound sentence =

A complex sentence =

How would you write it?

What word would you use?

Illustration © 2008 Moreno Chiacchiera

Metaphor generator

- Think about the different ideas listed below.

- Choose several of them, for example: an animal, a building, an emotion and a musical instrument.

- Select an example from each group that expresses you.

- Describe what each chosen object or idea might do and create some metaphors.

- Organise your best metaphors into a description.

- Here is one example:

Animal: I am a swan gliding at the edge of the lake.

Building: I am a skyscraper reflecting the sun.

Emotion: I am anger, red and on fire.

Musical instrument: I am a cymbal shivering in the dark.

I am:

a musical instrument	a TV show	a tool
a song/piece of music	a film	a tree
a book	a piece of art	a plant
an emotion	a building	a machine
a thought	a sport	a sound
an animal	a piece of furniture	a taste
a place	a type of transport	a sensation
a town/city/country	a body part	a temperature
a natural feature	a colour	a piece of electronic
a celebrity	a texture	equipment

Letter of complaint

Your address

Date

Dear Sir/Madam,

I am writing to complain about the current state of drawing pins produced by your company. As simple drawing pins they are fine, but what bothers me is that other office stationery products have evolved over the years, while your pins are the same as they were 100 years ago. As an example of creativity in other stationery products, I enclose a striped, plastic paper clip with a micro pencil inserted into one end. Your products are nothing like this.

Unless and until these matters are rectified, I shall be withholding any future purchase of drawing pins. As you know, my school is your biggest customer. Furthermore, might I recommend that you consider the following product innovations:

1.

2.

3.

4.

If you do not put matters right within two weeks I shall have no choice but to place my next order for 300,000,000 drawing pins with Zing Pins in China.

I await your response.

Yours faithfully,

Creativity contraption

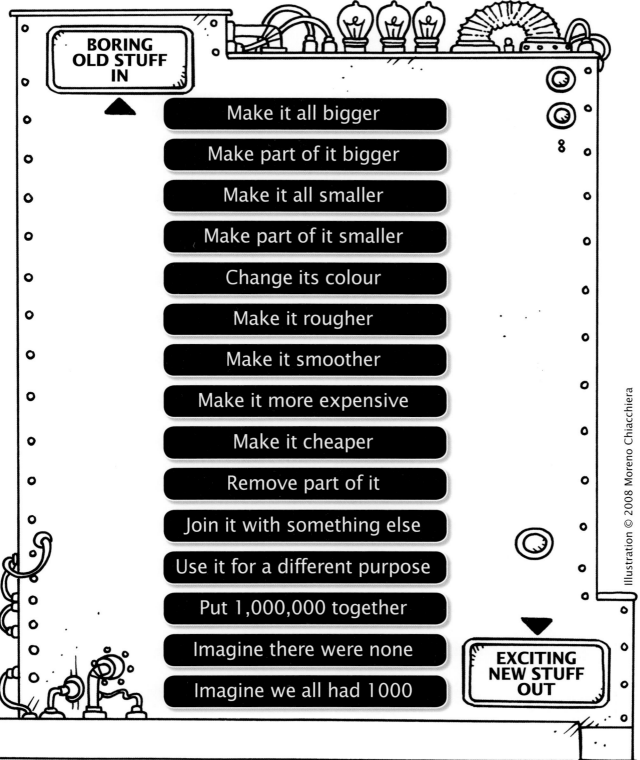

BORING OLD STUFF IN

- Make it all bigger
- Make part of it bigger
- Make it all smaller
- Make part of it smaller
- Change its colour
- Make it rougher
- Make it smoother
- Make it more expensive
- Make it cheaper
- Remove part of it
- Join it with something else
- Use it for a different purpose
- Put 1,000,000 together
- Imagine there were none
- Imagine we all had 1000

EXCITING NEW STUFF OUT

■SCHOLASTIC
www.scholastic.co.uk
PHOTOCOPIABLE Creative Activities for Thinking and Learning Skills: Ages 7-11

MI library

Smart Area

Fiction Books	Non-Fiction Books	Learning Resources

Floor Plan for _____ Smart Area

Fairy tale jigsaw

Character pieces

Big Bad Wolf	Cinderella	Three Little Pigs	Red Riding Hood	Hansel	Sleeping Beauty
Goldilocks	Jack	Elves	Shoemaker	Rumpelstiltskin	Rapunzel

Plot pieces

Stepmother tries to do away with

Bullied by sisters

Trying to guess a name

Secretly helping someone at night

Breaking into someone's cottage

Imprisoned in a tower

Pretending to be a grandma

Climbing up into the clouds

Setting pieces

A forest

A cottage

A beanstalk

A ballroom

A tower

A straw house

A castle

A bedroom

PHOTOCOPIABLE *Creative Activities for Thinking and Learning Skills: Ages 7-11*

Distant voices: communication ideas

Message rules

- should be less than ten words.
- must be clear and make sense.
- do not necessarily need to be written in sentences.
- should be fit for purpose.
- can be in text language but don't need to be.

Choose four communications from the list below and write appropriate text messages for each one. You could write to:

- Mikako, your girlfriend in space *(message will take 3 years to arrive)*
- yourself one year into the future
- yourself one year ago
- your first child
- your heart
- the Moon
- a starving boy
- God
- a fish in the sea
- time

- Noboru, your boyfriend on Earth *(message will take 3 years to arrive)*
- yourself ten years into the future
- your great-great-great-grandfather
- your first grandchild
- a star
- Earth
- a rich businessman
- your god
- the clouds
- water

1. _____

2. _____

3. _____

4. _____

SCHOLASTIC
www.scholastic.co.uk

Chapter Three

Thinking, learning, numeracy and science

- Creative Venn   48
- Oh dear! What can the matter be?   50
- What next?   52
- Tables speed dating   54
- Scream Park   56
- Biological plant   58
- Shapeshifter Betty   60

This chapter helps children to develop the thinking and learning skills introduced and learned in chapter one within the context of science and maths. Activities range from using Venn diagrams to designing a theme park ride.

● In the first activity, **Creative Venn**, children organise information into Venn diagrams. However, these are no ordinary Venn diagrams, but Venns with a twist that the children must work out how to use.

● In **Oh dear! What can the matter be?** children have to use their numeracy skills creatively and are required to put a numerical or monetary value on different crises and then decide which is the biggest.

● In **What next?** children explore patterns. Some patterns have been stolen from the numeracy vaults by artists, authors and sports people, and children must identify where they have been used. When getting to grips with the definition of a pattern, number and visual examples are a good place to start. But once children understand what patterns are, they will begin to find them everywhere!

● **Tables speed dating** helps children to explore different methods of remembering information. In this case, times tables facts. Children test out different methods of remembering by teaching each other in 'speed dating' style.

● In **Scream Park**, children work in groups to create a ride for a theme park. They must work together to design a ride that raises the pulse but also falls within budget.

● **Biological plant** requires children to design new animals that could potentially solve many of the problems that they have experienced. In this activity, they learn about the characteristics of different types of animal and develop their collaboration skills through working in teams and sharing knowledge.

● **Shapeshifter Betty** allows children to explore the features of different shapes while developing their problem-solving skills. The activity also teaches them how to deal with success and failure in competition. Children play 'Lucky Bridge', a game which requires them to match shapes which have one feature in common in order to find a way over Shapeshifter Betty's bridge.

Creative Venn

Setting the context
Venn diagrams are a simple way to organise and sort information. They were invented by a British mathematician called John Venn in 1881. It is a well-kept secret that John had a younger sister called Vanessa who was the black sheep of the family. She was a creative thinker and got into lots of trouble for messing around with her older brother's serious mathematical ideas. John's original diagram showed two circles overlapping. Objects with a particular feature are placed in the first circle; objects with another feature go in the second. Objects which have both features go in the overlap, and those with neither go completely outside both circles. But when Vanessa got hold of this simple idea, she added several imaginative twists…

The challenge
Can you work out how to use Vanessa's Venn diagrams? When you think you've cracked one of her ideas, try it out with some simple numbers and criteria.

Objectives
To learn to persevere in order to solve a problem.
To recognise problem-solving as a skill.
To explore how to use basic and extended Venn diagrams.
To practise organising information by applying criteria.

You will need
Some paper and pens or pencils; copies of photocopiable page 62. Create enough copies for the children to have one each and make an enlarged version to read and display at the front of the class.

Preparation
Choose a set of numbers and two sorting criteria with which to demonstrate a basic Venn diagram, for example, numbers 20–40 with the criteria being multiples of 8 and even numbers. You may want to prepare a copy of the 'Levels of success' chart opposite to dislay on a whiteboard or flipchart.

What to do
● Share the scenario with the children.
● Demonstrate a basic Venn diagram with your chosen set of numbers and simple criteria. Make sure you include numbers in all areas of the diagram: in the two separate circles, inside the overlap, and outside the circles altogether.
● With an air of mystery, reveal a page from the diary of Vanessa Venn and share one of the creative Venn diagrams with the children. Start with one of the more simple diagrams, such as the circle within a circle.
● Ask the children to discuss with a partner how this diagram could be used to sort information. Give an example of your own to start them off: for example, the outer circle could be numbers less than 10 and the inner circle could be even numbers.
● Discuss the children's ideas.
● Distribute copies of the diary page and ask the children to get into 'maths pairs' or organise them into pairs yourself by arranging the children into pairs who have similar mathematical ability and who can collaborate effectively.
● Tell them to try to discover the mysteries of at least two of Vanessa's diagrams and then test the solutions out with some simple numbers and criteria.
● Discuss and display the success criteria (see opposite).

Drawing together

● Ask some of the maths pairs to explain their conclusions about Vanessa's diagrams and demonstrate how they think the diagrams should be used.

● Ask the children these questions: *How difficult was the task? Did you ever consider giving up? If you chose to carry on, what made you? If you chose to give up, why did you? How did you feel when you worked out one of the diagrams? How did you feel when you got stuck? How did you go about solving the mystery of Vanessa's diagrams?*

● Discuss with the children the value of the skills and qualities needed to complete this activity successfully (such as problem solving, determination and patience). Consider how these would be useful in other areas.

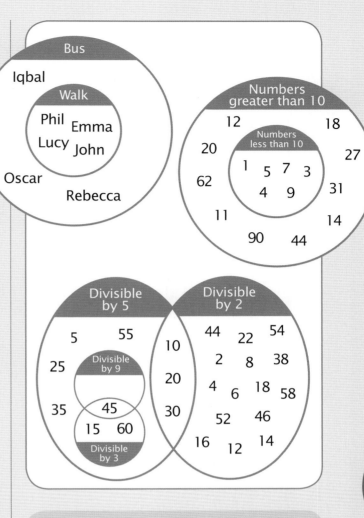

Extension

● Encourage more confident learners to look at the more complex of Vanessa's diagrams.

● Ask children to write their own page from Vanessa's diary where she adapts other mathematical ideas.

● Ask children to invent ways to apply the diagrams in different subjects, for example, sorting words in literacy or materials in science.

Support

● Pair children with those of similar mathematical/problem-solving ability.

● Direct children to Vanessa's more simple diagrams.

● Provide hints and suggestions, such as, *Try choosing four simple criteria and fitting them to a diagram.*

Page 49

Levels of success

Not there yet ☆	Nearly there ☆ ☆	Fantastic ☆ ☆ ☆
✔ Solution found for one or no diagrams	✔ Solution found for one or two diagrams	✔ Solution found for two or more diagrams
✔ Solution not tested to see if it works	✔ One solution proved to work through testing	✔ Two or more solutions proved to work
✔ Worked alone	✔ Worked well in pairs some of the time	✔ Worked well pairs: helped each other

Creative Activities for Thinking and Learning Skills: Ages 7-11

Oh dear!
What can the matter be?

Setting the context

'Oh no! I'm in trouble!' said Emma. She had borrowed her dad's watch and lost it.

'It's worse for me,' said Stephen. He had taken his sister shopping and left her in the bakery.

'You think you've got it bad?' said Paul. He had been playing in his dad's car, left the handbrake off and watched it crash into Mr Grice's new sports car.

'Not a patch on my crisis,' said Gemma. She had flushed her mum's credit cards and jewellery down the toilet.

'Mine's worse,' said Kyra. She had shouted 'Liar' really loudly at her sister. Her bedroom window was open, a passer-by misheard and within 10 minutes, three fire engines and 20 firefighters had arrived. Very soon they became three fire engines and 20 annoyed firefighters!

Everyone has a crisis now and again. And there's usually a price to pay. Crises can be sorted out but they can be expensive, not only in terms of money but in time and effort too. Crises are inevitable, so let's try to understand them.

The challenge

Develop a method for putting a numerical value on a crisis in order to decide which crisis is the biggest.

Objectives

To realise that every crisis can be resolved but that there is a cost.

To evaluate crises and compare their seriousness with one another.

To learn to apply mathematical thinking to real life.

You will need

Some rough paper; pens or pencils; whiteboards, draft boards or similar; a list of interesting crises – from personal to global. Some examples are listed below:

1. Someone left the bath tap running and the bath overflowed for 20 minutes.
2. Our car was stolen.
3. Half of the teachers were ill and were off school for a week.
4. My mum arrived at the supermarket checkout with a full trolley and discovered that she had no money.
5. I broke my leg in the playground.
6. Our house was burgled and my dad's computer was stolen.
7. Someone broke into the school and stole the computers.
8. 20cm of snow fell overnight.
9. The Government has banned the internet in school.
10. The school's heating is broken and it is a very cold day (minus 10 degrees Celsius).

Preparation

Choose a crisis that you have experienced and evaluate it in terms of its financial cost; the time taken to resolve it; the effort/emotional energy needed to sort it out. Begin to think about how time and effort can be given a monetary value. For example, 1 hour could equate to £60; a strong feeling of worry might cost £100 (these are arbitrary figures and the numbers that you and the children come up with will be used to develop their numeracy in an original way). If you prefer not to evaluate a crisis in monetary terms, take out the £ and create a scale. An example of how to put value on a crisis is outlined below:

Time: **Effort:**
1 hour = £100;   small: £10
                       medium: £50
                       large: £150
                       extra large: £500

Crisis 6
Financial cost: new window: £400
                     new computer: £1000

Time: 10 hours
(insurance claim, buying and installing a new computer, recovering files):
                10 x £100 = £1000

Effort: medium (insurance claim):   £50
           large (new computer): £150

400 + 1000 + 1000 + 50 + 150 =   £2600

Notional value of crisis 6 is £2600

What to do

● Read the context to the children and share a personal crisis with them.
● Ask the children to share their own crises (be sensitive to what might rise up to the surface here and be prepared to deal with things appropriately).
● Explain how you decided to put a value on the various aspects of your crisis (monetary or otherwise) and show the children how you calculated the value of the crisis.
● Tell them the value of an hour's effort and the cost of small, medium, large and extra large feelings (choose these figures so that the calculations that the children will be doing match their numeracy level. For example, one hour's effort could be worth £1 or £65.90).
● Select a crisis from the list and challenge

the children to estimate its value on their whiteboards, using the value figures that you suggest.
● Tell the children to work through each crisis in turn and find out which one is the biggest or most costly.

Drawing together

● Invite the children to work in pairs to compare their value for each crisis and encourage them to discuss the differences in their estimates.
● Attempt to reach a whole-class agreement on which crisis is the biggest.

Support

● Adapt the complexity of the crises and use simple numbers to value time/emotional effort.
● Pair less confident learners with those of stronger numerical ability.
● Focus on one or two crises only.

Extension

● Ask children to consider more positive life events – celebrations, successes, achievements and give value to them.
● Alter the numerical values of time and effort/emotion to make calculations more complex.
● Calculate a numerical value for local, national and global crises.

What next?

Setting the context

You are a team of investigative mathematicians called pattern detectives who have been asked by the World High Council of Maths to investigate recent thefts of valuable mathematical ideas. Reports have been coming in from field agents that other professional organisations have stolen patterns from the numeracy vaults, hidden deep in the secret Einstein caves. Mathematicians know that patterns are groups of numbers that repeat, loop around and join together according to rules. But it is believed that these ideas have been taken and used by artists, authors, geographers, musicians and even sports people.

The challenge

Using your knowledge of patterns, investigate other subjects to find out just how big the problem of pattern theft is.

Objectives

To apply knowledge of patterns in non-mathematical domains.
To discover patterns in art, language, music, sport and other subjects.
To expand personal definition of pattern.

You will need

Copies of photocopiable page 63, or make one large copy for display.

Preparation

Find and assemble a wide variety of patterns as suggested by the investigation worksheet, ready to look at and discuss with the children.

What to do

● Read the scenario to the children in the style of a secret communication (to James Bond, for example).
● Remind the children what a pattern is: a set of events, objects or ideas that repeats periodically. Numbers, shapes, sounds, actions, images and many other concepts can all be organised into a repeating sequence.
● Show the children a number pattern and then a pattern from nature (honeycomb, fish scales) and act as if it is horrific that patterns

have been stolen from the mathematicians.
● Invite the children to work in pairs to discover different places where the idea of a pattern has been used.
● Offer the children a range of ideas (as collected by the field agents on page 63) and discuss some specific examples such as a current pop song or hymn with repeating verses and choruses, a repetitive birdsong,

or a patterned part of the school uniform or the clothes you are wearing.

● Suggest that the children also think of other patterns that they have experienced – for example the pattern of day and night, the pattern of meals eaten, the pattern of their daily routine (when they get up, have lessons, go to bed and so on).

● Challenge them to find at least ten situations where patterns have been used 'illegally' and encourage them to explore different areas, rather than just focusing on ten examples from music.

Drawing together

● Call the pattern detectives back together to report on how serious the problem is.

● Ask them to share their findings and make a list together on a flipchart or whiteboard.

● Encourage the children to take on the role of secret agents reporting back to base (many of them will have watched TV programmes or films featuring secret agents, so they will know the routine).

● Can the children draw any conclusions from what they have found? Are patterns found more frequently in particular areas? Why do the children think that patterns appear so frequently in so many different areas of life?

Support

● Ask children to investigate more obvious patterns.

● Organise children into pairs who are able to support each other.

Extension

● Challenge children to combine patterns from different domains in innovative ways. For example, a number pattern mixed with a musical one might produce a song about numbers.

● Encourage them to create new patterns by continuing existing patterns in alternative ways. For example, by changing a pattern's existing colour, texture or size.

Tables speed dating

Setting the context

Quick recall of multiplication facts can help in problem-solving. If you can think of a multiplication fact quickly, you will spend less time on the basic calculations and more time thinking up a clever solution. But it can be difficult to learn lots of multiplication facts at once and some seem to be much more tricky to remember than others. Not to worry, help is at hand! Tables speed dating is a fun way to get to grips with troublesome times tables facts.

The challenge

Use 'Tables speed dating' to learn the times tables facts that you have always found difficult to remember.

Objectives

To learn and be able to recall at least three 'difficult' times tables facts.
To develop an effective way of teaching one fact to another person.
To develop independent working skills.

You will need

Multiplication squares for each child; a suitable space so that everyone in the group or class can stand in two lines, face to face with a partner.

Preparation

Organise for an area to be available as defined above.

What to do

● Ask the children to look at their multiplication square and identify three calculations that they find, or have found in the past, difficult to remember: 7 x 8 for example.
● Ask them to share and compare their choice with a partner. *Are there some times*

tables facts that everyone finds difficult?
● Now ask the children to think about how they remember things – in pictures in their heads, by saying things out loud, by association or as a rhythm and so on. Model different ways to recall a difficult times tables fact. For example 7 x 8 = 56 can be remembered by:
○ Noting that it includes 5, 6, 7, 8.
○ Imagining it in your head with a different colour for each number.
○ Saying it out loud (several times).
○ Making a memorable rhythm when saying it, '**S**e-ven **e**ights are **f**if-ty **s**ix'.
○ Relating it to people you know: I'm 8, John's 7, my gran is 56.
○ Making a story out of it: a 7-a-side football team scored 8 goals in their 56th match.
● Ask the children to each choose one difficult times tables fact and prepare to teach it to one other person. You may want to make a list on a flipchart or whiteboard of all the difficult facts that the children have chosen.

When this is done, arrange all the children into two straight lines facing each other with everyone having a partner.

Tell one line they are the teachers, the other line they are the learners.

Give the teacher line 30 seconds to teach their times tables fact to the learner opposite them.

After 30 seconds, tell the teachers to stop and ask them all to take one step sideways towards you so that they have a new partner. The child who no longer faces a partner walks quickly to the other end of the line, where there will be a space for them.

Tell the learners to repeat their teaching to their new partner.

After a further 30 seconds, repeat the sideways move.

After a couple more goes, swap the roles so the teachers become the learners and vice versa.

Repeat the activity.

Drawing together

Ask the children what they have learned and what they have taught.

If you made a list of multiplication facts that the children chose to teach, work through some of the facts and ask children to put up their hands if they now think that they know the answers. If appropriate, ask some children to give the answers to some of the facts.

Can the children draw any conclusion as to which methods of learning are most effective? Is there a general consensus or do different children prefer different methods? Has anyone learned a new method of learning that they had never tried before?

Support

Direct children to more simple tables facts or ask less confident learners to teach each other in pairs, rather than as a whole-class activity.

Extension

Challenge children to see how many different facts they can teach each other within a certain time limit.

Apply the speed dating technique in other subject areas.

Scream Park

Setting the context

Wide-Eye Designs is the top manufacturer of high-thrill roller coaster rides. Theme parks all around the world buy their rides from Wide-Eye and are forever demanding ones that are faster, longer and more scary. When theme parks ask for a new ride, Wide-Eye sends them a ride design pack which includes specifications for all the individual types of track – loops, twists, corners, straights and upside-downers. Each piece of track comes on a separate card with details of how much it affects the heart rate – this is a good measure of how frightening this part of the ride will be! The theme park then arranges the pieces into a new ride that they hope will provide lots of white-knuckle excitement for their thrill-seeking visitors, then Wide-Eye makes it.

The challenge

Your own company has just bought Scream Park, a failing theme park, and needs to invest in a winning roller coaster ride to attract customers back. Use the Wide-Eye ride design pack to create a high-thrill ride, bearing in mind your limited budget.

Objectives

To explore choices and make decisions through discussion with others.
To develop collaboration skills – fulfilling a specific role in a group.
To learn how numeracy skills can be applied to creative problem solving.

You will need

Two copies of photocopiable page 64 for each group of children; scissors; Blu-Tack®; glue.

Preparation

Familiarise yourself with the ride design pack to get an understanding of the various components. Use the internet to visit www.nolimitscoaster.com for free roller coaster simulations (note that a site licence is required for multiple users). Visit www.ukrides.info for photographs and film clips of rides in action around the world as well as maps of fairgrounds and theme parks. Write the design criteria (see 'What to do') on a flipchart or whiteboard to display during the lesson.

What to do

● Explain the scenario and problem to the children.
● If possible, show a roller coaster simulation or some video footage of someone on a ride.
● Arrange the children into groups of three or four and tell them to allocate the following group roles to those with the appropriate skills:

Facilitator – manages the group and makes sure everyone has a say in the discussions.
Builder – manages the materials, cutting, sticking and gluing.
Designer – manages ideas for the design.
Engineer – checks calculations.

Emphasise that although they have specific roles in the group, all members are expected to contribute ideas.
● Introduce the ride design pack (photocopiable page 64) and explain how it works. Different types of track can be fitted together depending on how much money is available and how scary the ride needs to be.
● Demonstrate fitting a loop to a straight and showing the overall cost and effect on

heart rate.

- Tell the children that while they are designing their roller coaster, you will be looking to see if they are sticking to their job roles and if groups are having good discussions: talking and listening well. Tell them that at the end of the lesson, as well as looking at their designs, you will share what you saw in terms of group work.

- Challenge the children to design a ride which adheres to the following rules:

  1. You have a budget of £1,000,000.
  2. Any track pieces can fit together in any order.
  3. There are 24 pieces available (two copies of the worksheet will provide 24 pieces).
  4. Heart rates at no time can go over 220 beats per minute (bpm).
  5. Assume an average starting heart rate of 90bpm.
  6. Think about the trade-off between cost/bpm and excitement!

Keep a record of the design criteria on a flipchart or whiteboard for the children to refer to throughout the lesson.

- As work commences, observe the groups and note down examples of what you consider to be the elements of good discussion (looking at the talker, turn-taking, responding to what is said) and job roles (not taking over other roles, fulfilling the task without being asked).

- Do not worry if not all (or none) of your expectations are met. The feedback of your observations to the children is the important thing. This will form a benchmark for their abilities in these two areas and can lead to targets for improvement.

Drawing together

- Ask pairs of groups to present their designs to each other. They should check each others' work against the design criteria.
- Instruct groups to check each others' calculations.
- Share your observations of group discussions and task roles.
- Ask the children what they now need to do to have better discussions and more effective task roles.

- Ask what gets in the way of improving discussion and task roles and what they can do about this.
- Record their answers publicly and refer to their suggestions next time good discussion or task roles are a focus.

Support

- Carefully allocate roles and organise the children into groups to facilitate successful group work.
- Adapt the numbers used on the ride design sheet and the budget allowed according to the skills of the class.

Extension

- Organise children into larger groups with additional task roles (presenter, salesperson and so on).
- Adapt the numbers in the ride design pack so that they are larger or include decimals.
- Ask children to create new track options.
- Challenge children to create two or more options for a roller coaster ride within the same budget and then evaluate which is the best and why.

Biological plant

Setting the context

Over recent years, scientists have discovered a great deal about how living things are made. They explore life itself and use their findings to help cure diseases and improve the quality of life for many people. Scientists can genetically modify plants, clone animals and they have also started to combine human and animal cells. In the right hands, these ideas could save the planet; in the wrong ones, it could be destroyed. Dr Gene is a scientist working in a biological plant. In his laboratory he has discovered how to combine any living thing with any other and he is using this knowledge to design new plants and animals to help solve the many problems faced by Earth such as pollution, crime, overcrowding and climate change.

The challenge

As genetic engineers, help Dr Gene to explore the key features of different living things and then combine several of their characteristics to solve specific problems.

Objectives

To develop collaboration skills.
To explore how to synthesise an original living thing to meet a specific requirement.
To know and understand several key facts about plants and animals.

You will need

Flipchart paper and marker pens for groups of five children.

Preparation

The children will be using a 'carousel' activity to generate their ideas, so you will need to arrange your teaching space so that groups of five can move easily between different carousel stations (tables) with a flipchart page of questions. At the top of each flipchart page, write a key question. You will need a different page for each group but questions can be repeated. They can relate directly to aspects of the science curriculum or remain fairly generic. For example: What do animals have? (eyes, spines, fur, paws...)

What do animals do? (run, bite, jump, kill, give birth, fly...) What do plants have? (leaves, roots, stigma, bark...) What do plants do? (take in CO_2, grow, give fruit...) What problems does the world face? (pollution, population growth...) What local problems do we face? (litter, safety, noise...) Prepare the carousel rules on a flipchart or whiteboard (rules are outlined in 'What to do'). In addition, create an ' Levels of success' chart for the children to use to evaluate their work at the end of the activity.

What to do

● Read the context and problem to the children and share anecdotes such as Dolly the cloned sheep, mapping of the human genome, GM foods and so on.
● Cast the children in the roles of genetic engineers who work at the biological plant.
● Ask them to get into groups of five and choose a facilitator and a scribe.
● Explain the carousel rules to the children, pointing them out on the flipchart or

whiteboard as you talk about them:

1. Write answers to the question on the flipchart page on the table.
2. The facilitator should make sure everyone's ideas are written down.
3. After 1–2 minutes, all groups move in the same direction to the question on the next table. (You will say when to move.)
4. Change the role of scribe.
5. Read the answers that have already been written on the flipchart page and put a dot next to the ones you like the best.
6. Add more answers of your own.
7. After time is called, move to the next station, changing the scribe role and repeating the activity again.

● Make sure that you visit each question and add key ideas that the children may have missed.
● When all groups have had the chance to answer all of the questions, bring the children back together and Blu-Tack® the flipchart pages around the classroom.
● Tell the children to use the collected ideas to genetically engineer a new living thing that will solve a problem. They should choose a problem from the relevant flipchart page, and then select features from the other pages.
● Share the following as an example (or use the children's ideas). Problem: noisy night-time neighbours. Solution: a dog with bat's ears, peacock's feathers and cockerel's voice can detect where the night-time noise is coming from, silently shelter you with a fan of feathers, and make horrendous noise itself until the neighbours quieten down.

Drawing together
● Ask the children in pairs to present their new creations to each other.
● Select a couple of children to present to the class and note how the carousel ideas have been used. Find out who contributed the ideas to the carousel to show how one person's thinking can help another.
● Invite the children to self-assess their work according to the success criteria that you drew up earlier. How successful do they think they were as genetic engineers?

Support
Give some children suggestions for simple problems and a less abstract starting point such as cats getting lost.

Extension
● Put two or more new creations together and ask children to anticipate how they would interact.
● Start with a new living thing and challenge children to work out what other problems it could solve.
● Repeat the carousel with more specific questions (for example, living things found in a garden).
● Represent creations by drawing or modelling.

Shapeshifter Betty

Setting the context

Your quest is almost over; your tasks are nearly complete. You have slain Grub Spike, the pin-headed monster, rescued Princess Emma from the clutches of the Stretch Twins, wrestled the priceless Orb of Thought from the evil Qua-Man of Hobblebrook and climbed the infamous Cheese Mountain. Maybe now your father will accept you as someone with great courage? Only one thing now stands between you and your triumphant return to the village: Lucky Bridge. Lucky Bridge is guarded by a shapeshifter called Betty. You must outwit her to cross the bridge safely. Make one false move and you will discover very quickly what flying without wings feels like.

The challenge

To cross Lucky Bridge, you must build a route that takes you safely from one side of the bridge to the other. While you're trying to make your way across, Betty will try to stop you. Out-think her if you can!

Objectives

To learn to accept defeat and success appropriately when competing in a game.
To explore strategies to solve and adapt a mathematical puzzle.
To use accurate shape vocabulary.

You will need

A copy of the gameboard and pieces from photocopiable pages 65 and 66, photocopied onto card, for pairs of children to play.

Preparation

Cut out the shape pieces and sort them into packs. In each pack, half of the pieces should be on different-coloured card. Practise playing the game yourself to understand how it works. Write out a list of the game rules for the children to refer to (see 'What to do'). Prepare a 'Level of success' chart opposite for display on a whiteboard or flipchart.

What to do

● Describe the scenario to the children.
● Demonstrate how to play the Lucky Bridge game and explain the following rules:
    1. Shapes come in large, medium and small sizes with a number 1, 2, 3 or 4 on them.
    2. Shuffle and deal the shape cards: each player is given different-coloured cards.
    3. Players take turns to place shape pieces next to each other.
    4. Players must always place a piece next to one that is already on the bridge.
    5. A piece must share one feature (size, shape or number) with all of its neighbours.
    6. Player 1 tries to make a route across the bridge.
    7. Player 2 (Betty) tries to block the route. She wants to prevent Player 1 from getting even part of the way across the bridge.

- Ask the children what good, competitive game play looks like and sounds like.
- Collect and record their ideas in a list. (Good competitive game play should show children taking turns, accepting defeat in a mature way, congratulating the winner, saying 'Well played' to each other and so on.
- Distribute the gameboard, pieces and rules to each pair and let them begin to play.
- Observe the children playing; check their behaviour against the good game play list.

Drawing together
- Ask the children what strategies they developed (for example, Player 1 observing which shape pieces Betty has in order to plan a sequence of moves in advance) and discuss how well they stuck to good game play.
- Encourage the children to evaluate the game itself. Ask them if the game is 'fair' and discuss the rules that could be changed or added to improve it: for example, reducing the number of pieces or the features that neighbouring shapes must share. Some children may query why Betty wouldn't just block the top of the bridge; or there may have been disputes over whether diagonal counts as 'next to each other'.

Lucky Bridge game

Betty this side

Cross this way

Illustration © 2008 Moreno Chiacchiera

Page 65

Extension
- Alter the shape of the gameboard.
- Invent new pieces: words, animals, sounds, all of which need to have some shared common features.
- Invite children to play in teams and discuss their moves.

Support
Pair children appropriately and alter the rules, the size of the gameboard or the number of variables in the game pieces.

Levels of success

Not there yet ☆	Nearly there ☆☆	Fantastic ☆☆☆
✔ Showed poor sportsmanship: eg did not take turns or did not congratulate the winner	✔ Showed good sportsmanship most of the time: eg took turns but unfriendly at the end	✔ Showed good sportsmanship all the time: took turns, said 'well done at the end', accepted defeat
✔ Matched some shapes and numbers correctly	✔ Matched most shapes and numbers correctly	✔ Matched all shapes and numbers correctly

Vanessa Venn's diary

15th December 1881

Found one of J.'s notebooks today – all neat and tidy like usual. Tore out a page (oops)! He'd drawn two circles on it. Some type of sorting thingy. Good idea, but he stopped there and didn't develop his idea. What a waste! So I've helped him along. Hope he doesn't nick my thoughts. Best hide this away in the 'secret place'. Rained all day. Had steak pie for tea.

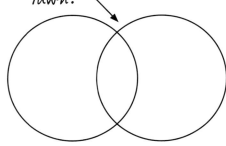

John's idea for sorting. Yawn.

Vanessa's super, excellent better-than-John's ideas for sorting stuff

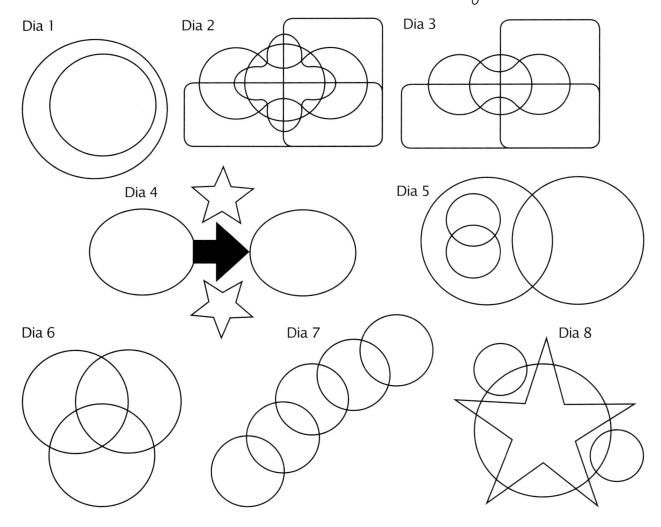

Dia 1 Dia 2 Dia 3 Dia 4 Dia 5 Dia 6 Dia 7 Dia 8

Patterns investigation worksheet

File Ref: 071107

Spook 007

Operation: Pattern theft

Leads from: Field agents

Suspicious activity observed in:

- music on the radio
- sounds outside
- sounds that people make
- poems read aloud
- humans talking
- animal sounds, especially dogs
- times of day
- trains and buses
- sports clothing
- animal coverings – skin, fur
- plants – leaves, bark, flowers
- crowds of humans
- buildings
- furniture
- libraries
- shops
- streets
- parks

Action: Investigate all leads

Top Priority: Stealth and secrecy essential

Wide-Eye ride design pack

Straight Horizontal
Cost £35,000
Heart rate -20bpm

Straight Horizontal
Cost £35,000
Heart rate -20bpm

Vertical Drop Cost £55,000
Heart rate +37bpm

Vertical Loop Cost £155,000
Heart rate +25bpm

Spiral
Cost £91,000
Heart rate +42bpm

Vertical Loop
Cost £155,000
Heart rate +25bpm

Slow-down Straight
Cost £42,000
Heart rate -30bpm

Very Sharp Corner
Cost £38,000
Heart rate +15bpm

Gentle Corner
Cost £31,000
Heart rate -18bpm

Spiral
Cost £91,000
Heart rate +10bpm

Vertical Fall
Cost £89,000
Heart rate +45bpm

Powered Straight
Cost £31,000
Heart rate +37bpm

Illustration © 2008 Moreno Chiacchiera

■SCHOLASTIC
www.scholastic.co.uk

Lucky Bridge game

Betty this side

Cross this way

Page 65

Betty's Bridge pieces

Chapter Four

Thinking, learning and the humanities

- So what if...   68
- Time tunnel   70
- Ultimate town
  planner   72

The three activities in this chapter allow children to practise and improve their thinking and learning skills in the contexts of history or geography.

The first task, **So what if...** gives children the opportunity to think creatively about history, while consolidating their knowledge of history topics already studied. In this activity they are required to imagine what could have happened if certain significant events from the past hadn't happened and the impact this could have had on their own lives.

Time tunnel is also history-based and requires children to work in a large group. The task requires all children to find a historical fact and repeat it as they take turns to enter the time tunnel. It may sound a simple enough task but there are rules to be adhered to and time limits imposed. For it to be a success, this activity requires high levels of cooperation and maturity from children. It is quite feasible for KS2 children to complete it successfully, but they need to have worked up to it through previous experience of activities requiring collaboration with partners and small groups. It is a high-risk activity, but whatever the outcome, your feedback to the children will have great learning value.

In **Ultimate town planner**, children work in groups to design a perfect town: a place with enough space for everyone, safe cycling routes, no pollution and so on. However, they must work to just ten design criteria and so must learn to prioritise, collaborate and compromise within their group.

So what if...

Setting the context

Books and films often encourage us to imagine what would have happened if certain key events in history hadn't occurred or if they had played out differently. What if dinosaurs hadn't died out? What if Henry VIII had stayed Catholic? What if Charles Babbage had put his energies into gardening rather than computing? It is very interesting to speculate about such things and it can help you to make better decisions in your own life. Let's take some ideas from history and play around with them by asking 'So what if...'

The challenge

Imagine what consequences there might have been for the present if certain events in history had been different.

Objectives

To develop enquiry skills.
To explore how ideas connect together in terms of cause and effect.
To consolidate understanding of a range of historical facts.

You will need

A variety of historical text books and access to other historical material via the internet, DVDs or CDs that covers history topics that the children have recently learned about at school; the children's current and past history work; some small pieces of card – two pieces per child.

Preparation

Create a resource area in the classroom that gives children free access to a wide range of historical information. Include their own history books, projects or specific pieces of work.

What to do

● Explain to the children the concept of 'So what if...' and give a few examples.
● Start locally (in terms of time and space): 1. So what if my car had been stolen last week? (I would have had to sort it out, spending time filling in an insurance form; I would have had less time to plan lessons; my lessons might have been more spontaneous but would have been badly organised; I might not have been able to get to school; the children might have had a cover teacher.) 2. So what if the shop had had no milk this morning? (I would have had nothing for breakfast as there would have been no milk for my cereal; I would have been extremely hungry and unable to concentrate; I would have become irritable and angry when I shouldn't have been.)

● Ask the children to think up a simple, personal 'So what if...' based on an event from last week and invite them to tell a partner what the consequence *right now* might be.

● Share an historical 'So what if' related to your current history topic. Make sure a consequence can be traced right the way to the present day. For example, if Henry VIII hadn't been allowed a divorce, Elizabeth I wouldn't have been born; whoever ruled instead of her might not have been so successful; we might not have defeated the Spanish Armada and we might still be living under Spanish rule!

● Once you feel that the children understand the concept, ask them to go to the resource area and give each child two small pieces of card.

● Set them the task of creating a 'So what if... Here's what' scenario, working independently. Start by asking them to look

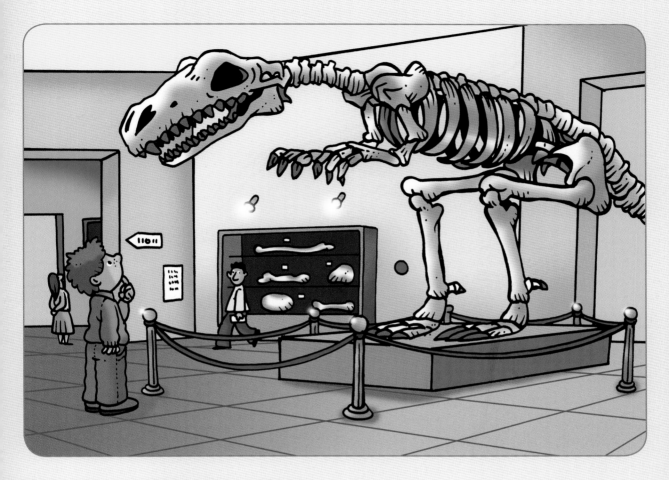

through the resources to choose an historical event and then ask: *So what if it was different in some way?* Tell them to record their revised event on a small piece of card. Challenge them to think about how this event might make a difference to life today and answer the prompt: 'Here's what...' They should record the 'Here's what...' idea on their other piece of card.

Drawing together
- Bring the children back together.
- Ask them to turn and sit with two other people and share their cards.
- Then ask the children in their threes to put their six cards together, mix them up and hand them to another three.
- Threes now match up each 'So what if...' card to the correct 'Here's what...' card.
- Ask the children to describe their thinking: How were they able to connect different pasts to different present days? Use the following questions: *Is it an easy task? What sort of thinking is it? What have you learned from this task about history or about creative thinking?*

Support
- Direct children towards more familiar historical events with more obvious present day consequences. Events that happened more recently are often easier to relate to the present.
- Use familiar, personal, past events, rather than wider historical events.
- Allow children to work in pairs.

Extension
- Speculate about the future: how would a 'So what if...' now affect 20 years into the future?
- Speculate back from the future. Imagine a future event and then work backwards to discover what needs to happen now to cause the future event.

Time tunnel

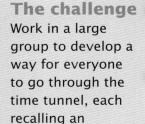

Setting the context
The time tunnel is a clever device to help people learn lots of interesting facts from history. However, it is a tricky machine to use and we must follow the rules carefully when it is switched on. It only works properly when a large number of people use it at the same time and this can cause big challenges with cooperation. And it requires such a lot of energy that it can only be switched on for short periods of time, so you'll be working under pressure too.

The challenge
Work in a large group to develop a way for everyone to go through the time tunnel, each recalling an interesting historical fact.

Objectives
To explore and develop cooperation skills when working under time pressure within a large group.
To consolidate historical knowledge.
To develop skills at summarising information.

You will need
A variety of historical text books and access to other historical material via the internet, DVDs or CDs that cover history topics that the children will be familiar with; the children's current and past history work; one small piece of card for each child; a large PE hoop or similar; a method of timing accurately to the second.

Preparation
You will need access to a large, open area such as the school hall or playground. Display the time tunnel rules (see 'What to do') on a flipchart or a whiteboard. You may also like to have a copy of the 'Levels of success' chart opposite on display.

What to do
● Introduce the activity to the children.
● Give them ten minutes to each find an interesting historical fact using the resources provided and ask them to write their fact on a piece of card, using less than ten words.
● Take the children to the open area and ask them to stand in a circle.
● Introduce the time tunnel (hoop) and share the following rules:
  1. Everyone must go right through the time tunnel only once.
  2. Each person must say their interesting fact as they go through the tunnel.
  3. Everyone must have a different fact.
  4. Everyone should listen to each others' facts.
  5. The time tunnel can only be switched on for 75 seconds at a time – so everyone must go through within that time.
  6. It takes two minutes to cool down before you can try again.
● Step back, set a 15-minute time limit and let the children start.
● Use your professional judgement as to when and how you intervene in ways other than timing their attempts and the time tunnel cooling period.
● As long as the children's interactions are safe and respectful you will gather a great deal of priceless information – even if they

don't complete the task.
- As you observe, focus on the following: Who steps forward as the leader? Who takes a back seat? Who has the ideas? Who suggests alternatives? Who enjoys it? Who hates it? Who disengages? Who helps others? Who notices the time?
- Take digital photos of the task.

Drawing together
- At a suitable point, bring the activity to a close and ask the children to share three historical facts that they have learned in the last 15 minutes.
- Discuss the children's experiences of the time tunnel using questions such as: *Do you learn more under pressure? Did you enjoy*

the time tunnel? Were everyone's ideas heard? What have you learned about learning historical facts? What have you learned about working in a large group under time pressure?
- Record key responses and reframe them as targets for the next large group task.

Support
- Make suggestions and give encouragement throughout the activity.
- Alter the time tunnel rules, for example, by extending the time.
- Split the class into two halves, or smaller groups, if necessary.

Extension
Provide a tunnel that is more awkward to get through (make it smaller or out of elastic or string).

Levels of success

Not there yet ⭐	Nearly there ⭐⭐	Fantastic ⭐⭐⭐
✔ Many facts said twice	✔ Some facts said twice	✔ All facts were different
✔ Over half the class went through the hoop	✔ Most of the class went through the hoop	✔ All of the class went through the hoop
✔ Listened some of the time	✔ Listened most of the time	✔ Listened all of the time

Ultimate town planner

Setting the context

The government has decided to build a new town called Belly Kalls. They want it to be right in the middle of the countryside and to feature the best in urban design. One hundred thousand people will live there in harmony. All the problems of current town planning will have been designed out. There will be enough space for everyone, safe cycling routes and play areas for children. There will be reduced pollution, plenty for everyone to do, clean streets, quiet neighbourhoods and much more!

The challenge

Working as urban design teams, make a visual plan for Belly Kalls. Each team member should contribute his or her best ideas to the group plan.

Objectives

To identify the key features of a successful small town.
To develop collaboration and listening skills while taking a specific role in a team.
To develop presentation skills.

You will need

Aerial photographs of small towns; access to Google Earth™ mapping service www.earth. google.com and copies of photocopiable page 74 for each urban design team.

Preparation

Make a list of the features that you expect to see in the children's designs (see the examples given on photocopiable page 74). Collect together some visual resources that show these features (such as an aerial photo of an open space to show a playground or sports field, pictures of factories, stations, swimming pools and so on).

What to do

- Read the scenario to the children.
- Arrange them into urban design teams with the following task roles: Facilitator – manages the team; Chief designer – collects ideas; Project manager – manages time and resources; Spokesperson – presents ideas to other people outside the team.
- Ask each design team to examine the source material and come up with a list of ten things that they think need to be in Belly Kalls. They could use photocopiable page 74 to help generate ideas.
- Ask them to decide, as a group, which are their top five items on the list.
- Bring the teams back together as a whole class and ask the spokesperson for each group to share one item from their top five.
- Record these on a flipchart or whiteboard and continue until you have a list of ten.
- Give teams 30 minutes to create a town plan that fulfils the agreed criteria set as a class. Make sure that the children are aware that at the end of the lesson their spokesperson will need to present their ideas to the class.
- Ensure that each team member remembers their role: Facilitator – manages the team by making sure that everyone is doing their job; Chief designer – asks for and records each person's ideas in turn; Project

manager – informs the team about time and gets anything that is needed (paper and so on); Spokesperson – prepares to tell other teams about the design at the end of the lesson.

Drawing together

● Bring the design teams back together as a class and listen to their presentations.

● The other teams should listen and check that the presented plan meets the ten criteria.

● Display all the plans and tell the children to look at them individually. They should decide what is good about the plans and write positive comments on Post-it Notes®, sticking them next to the relevant place on each plan.

Support

Simplify the town requirements or reduce the number of requirements to five and organise children into appropriate teams.

Extension

● Two teams should get together and create a new plan by combining the best features of each of their plans.

● Ask children to plan a city, a country or a planet.

Ultimate town planner

- Here are some ideas to get you started with your design for Belly Kalls. You might want your new town to have:

open green spaces

houses for single people, couples, families and older people

safe cycling routes

plenty of shops

factories away from houses

safe residential areas

leisure centres

play parks

a railway station

a sensible road design

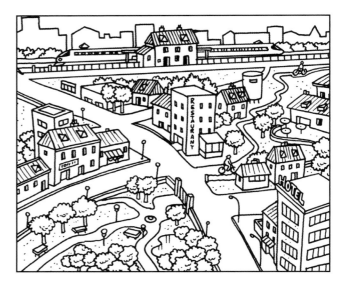

- Now think of some ideas of your own.

_____

_____

_____

_____

_____

- As a group, decide which are your five best ideas. Write them here.

_____

_____

_____

Illustration © 2008 Moreno Chiacchiera

■SCHOLASTIC
www.scholastic.co.uk

Chapter Five

Thinking, learning and the creative arts

- What's the score? 76
- Class profile 78
- Creative meditation 80
- Learning tableau 82
- Painting by numbers 84

The five activities in this chapter develop thinking and learning skills in the contexts of music, art and crafts.

● In **What's the score?** children create a composition using just their bodies and one percussion instrument. Through this activity they explore the role of a conductor and the purpose of a music score, while developing their performance, creative thinking and problem-solving skills at the same time.

● The second and third activities, **Class profile** and **Creative meditation** both require children to combine ICT and creative thinking skills. In **Class profile**, children employ their ICT, creative and self-evaluation skills to make simple audio files about themselves. Children's individual work is then brought together to make a comprehensive online class file. In **Creative meditation**, the teachers at school are feeling very stressed and have asked the children to help them relax! They do this by creating short PowerPoint® presentations comprising soothing and peaceful images, music and sound effects.

● **Learning tableau** is a drama-based activity through which children create a tableau, mime or silent role play to demonstrate the value of thinking and learning skills to pupils at a different school who have yet to learn their benefits.

● In **Painting by numbers**, children develop their drawing and collage skills by creating a piece of artwork for an international holiday company, Hotel Spin. However, the holiday company has made some tough demands and each piece of artwork must fulfil specific requirements – most of which are decided by the role of a dice!

What's the score?

Setting the context

Every successful and talented musician knows how important it is to be able to follow a musical score. A musical score is a set of instructions which tells a band of musicians what to do and when to do it. The conductor of the band points and waves his baton to help the musicians keep time and follow the score correctly. Your band, 'Body Part Harmonies' has a concert tonight and you are about to go on stage! Well, you would be if someone hadn't stolen all your instruments and the score... But the show must go on and you're going to do whatever it takes to give the audience the performance of a lifetime!

The challenge

In a small group, create a graphic score for a piece of music that only uses one musical instrument and your own bodies.

Objectives

To develop organisation skills, arranging ideas into an effective order.
To contribute a unique musical part to an original piece.
To explore the role of a conductor.

You will need

A selection of tuned and untuned percussion instruments (one instrument for each group of five); a flipchart page, a marker pen and a real baton (or alternative) for each group of five.

Preparation

Prepare your own simple graphic score – or use photocopiable page 86. Enlarge the score for display or make a copy for each group. Use a flipchart or whiteboard to display the criteria for a graphic score that the children must include (see 'What to do').

What to do

● Share the scenario with the children and discuss possible solutions to the problem.
● Show them the limited number of

Tambourines and Music Stand © 2008 JupiterImages Corporation instruments available and demonstrate a variety of body and voice sounds, such as clapping, stamping, hissing, or making 'ah' and 'ooh' sounds.

● Select several children to help you demonstrate the graphic score you prepared earlier (or the one from page 86), with each child taking one part. With you as the conductor, move your baton very slowly from left to right across the score. The musicians follow their line and make their sounds when the baton is at the right place. For example, the 'ahhh' makes her sound when the baton moves in line with the horizontal black lines. The height of the black line in the box indicates the pitch of the note.

● Organise the children into groups of five and give them 20 minutes to create a similar graphic score according to the criteria below. Make sure this list is on display for the children to refer to throughout the activity.

    1. Everyone must be involved in the performance.
    2. Only one person should conduct.
    3. Only one percussion instrument is allowed.
    4. Each person should make a different sound from their mouth or with another part of their body.
    5. The piece is to last no longer than 20 seconds.
    6. The score must be recorded on flip chart paper in the style of the example shown.

Drawing together

● Give the groups time to practise and then listen to each group perform their composition. Children should assess each other by referring to the criteria listed at the start of the activity.

● Ask the groups to perform again and, this time, tell the conductors to speed up or slow down the performances.

● Place several scores together and play them one after the other or simultaneously.

● Discuss the children's experience. Consider the following questions: *Did you follow the directions of your conductor? How did the conductor help the performance when you had to play at a different pace? Did each*

person in your group contribute a unique sound? How could the performance be improved? Did you work well together in your groups?

Support

● Provide children with a score to follow – or a partially created score for them to finish.

● Provide a list of sounds for children to choose from.

Extension

● Ask children to create a score for a particular purpose: for a film soundtrack or to suggest a particular mood.

● Tell the conductors to conduct the scores at different speeds and backwards.

● Have more than one person making each sound and create a whole-class performance.

● More confident learners could create a graphic score for a short video clip.

Class profile

Speakers © 2008 JupiterImages Corporation

Setting the context
The internet offers us some wonderful free programs and resources, doesn't it? There are free sound recorders and editors, and forums where people of similar professions can exchange ideas and share photographs, film clips and other resources. If we want to be truly successful in the 21st century, then we need to have mastery of ICT and the internet. We have to be able to find the software tools that we need to help us learn and work effectively. Let's start by creating our own class Wikispace to creatively express our learning, success and targets.

The challenge
Create an on-line class profile that includes audio sound files.

Objectives
To develop teamwork skills by contributing to a whole-class project.
To evaluate own thinking and learning in terms of successes and targets.
To learn how to use an audio recorder and web page creatively and effectively.

You will need
Whole-class access to the internet; a sound recorder installed on class computers (Audacity, for example, which can be downloaded from http://audacity. sourceforge.net; an account on a forum page such as Wiki and class space set up with a page for each pupil see www.wikispaces. com; a microphone for each computer.

Preparation
Learn how to set up and manage your online space – this is an extremely straightforward and intuitive process. Download and learn to use your recording software – again this is very easy to do. Record and upload a sound file in which you respond to the following learning prompts:
  ○ Recently I've learned to…
  ○ What I want to learn next is…
  ○ I learn best when I can…
In a preceding ICT session, introduce children to the sound recorder and let them explore its features. Prior to the session, ensure that each child is able to record their voice and save the file as an .MP3 or .WAV.

What to do
● Organise the children into pairs at computers.
● Tell them to work together because they will be learning to use some powerful software.
● During an ICT session, when all the children have access to a computer and the internet, introduce the class Wikispace and show them your page.
● Listen to the sound file you have recorded on the page.
● Share the three learning prompts (see Preparation) and tell the children to prepare their responses.
● Allow the children to use the sound recorder to record their responses and save the file to their personal folders.
● Demonstrate how to navigate to their Wiki page and how to upload a file.
● Tell them to upload their audio file to their page.

Drawing together
● Allow the children to listen to each others' sound files. Have they discovered anything new about themselves or their classmates?
● Ask the children to describe any technical difficulties that they encountered and ask

how these problems were solved: did they work independently or collaboratively to overcome obstacles?

● Discuss the value of websites such as these and emphasise the importance of using the internet responsibly (not meeting strangers from internet sites or chat rooms, being careful about the types of photographs and information they are allowing other people to access and so on.)

Support
● Pair less confident learners with those who are more articulate, more self-aware of learning behaviour or more technically competent.
● Provide children with a 'welcome' sound file to upload that you have pre-recorded, instead of asking them to record their own material.

Extension
● Develop individual Wikispaces by adding images (be aware of your school's internet policy here), further learning diary entries, links, video clips and so on.
● Create subject-based Wikispaces.
● Create different areas for learning skills and thinking skills.

Creative meditation

Setting the context

Learning, teaching and life inside and outside school can be very stressful, especially for teachers! Short, regular relaxation and meditation sessions can help keep people calm and reduce anxiety. Your teachers have come to you for help. They want quick and easy ways to relax at playtime so that they feel refreshed when they return to the classroom to teach you. They appreciate relaxing sounds and soothing images and like nothing better than a short, tranquil PowerPoint® slideshow (especially those that include music and nice pictures) to put their feet up to during playtime.

The challenge

Design a relaxation PowerPoint® slideshow for stressed teachers.

Objectives

To learn that the brain and body need regular, focused down time to be able to work and learn effectively.

To develop qualities of consideration and understanding – thinking about what another person might be thinking.

To explore how to combine pictures and sounds creatively in a multimedia presentation.

You will need

All children will need access to computers with presentational software such as PowerPoint® installed, as well as access to digital images and relaxation music. Photographs could be those you or the children have taken, or images from resources such as www.iStockphoto.com, www.fotosearch.com or www.flickr.com (copyright permitting).Children should be supervised when using these sites to ensure content being accessed is suitable. Sample music is often provided on computer hard drives or you could record your own relaxing sounds (such as running water, the wind, or birds singing).

Preparation

Create your own PowerPoint® slideshow of relaxing images (mountains, rivers, pastel colours and so on). Set up slow, automatic slide transition and add relaxation music to play during the show. Before you begin the activity, ensure that all children know how to use the free image download site on the internet (if you are using one) and how to find, open and save files on a computer. All children will also need to be familiar with the basics of how to use PowerPoint®, knowing how to:

- ○ add new slides
- ○ add images to slides
- ○ add transitions between slides
- ○ add music
- ○ set it to play for a number of slides.

What to do

● Immediately after playtime or lunch break, show the children your PowerPoint® relaxation show. Ask them to become aware of their breathing as they watch it and maybe to slow it down a little. Discuss why you have chosen particular resources and ask the children to suggest other ideas of images

and sounds that people find relaxing.
● Demonstrate how you created your slideshow, reminding the children how to add slides, images, transitions and music or sounds. Experiment with different transitions and sounds and discuss any that are particularly relaxing or not relaxing.
● Give the children computer access to PowerPoint®, either in a computer suite or using laptops. Provide some images and some relaxation music. Children can work individually or in pairs depending on the resources available.
● Ask them to create a relaxation show to fulfil these success criteria:
  1. The slideshow should include at least seven relaxing images.
  2. There should be appropriate transitions between images.
  3. There should be appropriate music playing throughout (or sound effects if the children prefer).
  4. The slideshow should play automatically and should last between one and two minutes
  5. It should help stressed teachers to relax.

© Corel

Page
81

Drawing together
● Showcase several of the children's PowerPoint® presentations and ask the class to assess them against the criteria. Which one do the children think is most relaxing and why?
● Make the slideshows available to colleagues in the staffroom and ask them for their feedback. Share your colleagues' responses with the children.
● Suggest to the children that they can use the shows for their own relaxation if they feel stressed (during SATs perhaps!).

Support
● Pair less confident children with others who have more advanced ICT skills or have a greater understanding of stress and the need to relax.
● Make the task easier by allowing children to add to your PowerPoint® slideshow instead of creating their own from scratch.

Extension
Suggest that more confident children add encouraging and inspiring text to some of the images, or challenge them to animate the text appropriately.

Learning tableau

Setting the context

In this class, we are very lucky. Not only do we explore many different subjects, but we have been learning to learn and learning to think. Not everyone gets these opportunities. The children of Woody Vale certainly don't. They don't speak our language and they have to sit in rows all day long copying from the board. We've got a chance to explain to them how we've been learning but we can't use words because they wouldn't be able to understand what we're saying. We'll have to use mime, silent role play and tableau.

The challenge

Create a short, silent dramatic piece that expresses your learning styles, thinking skills and dreams for the future and shows how these are all connected.

Objectives

To develop group-work skills.
To explore and reflect on learning styles and thinking skills.
To learn to express dreams and aspirations through drama.

You will need

A large space for drama work: the school hall, or playground for example; a video camera and permission from parents/ carers for children to be filmed; copies of photocopiable page 87.

Preparation

Think about possible actions, poses and movements that could be used to describe aspects of learning styles and thinking skills. Perhaps try out a few in front of a mirror to ensure that you are confident in demonstrating these to the class. You may want to prepare a chart of the five criteria listed in the 'What to do' section and display this on a flipchart.

What to do

● As a drama warm-up, call out words from the Learning tableau worksheet on page 87.
● Challenge the children to respond to each word by striking a pose, making a face or both. For example: *Be cold* could be shivering and screwing up your face; *Ask a question* could be putting a hand in the air with eyebrows raised; *Remember* could be putting a finger to your temple and frowning.
● Explain the scenario to the children.
● Ask them to get into groups of three or four and to prepare a silent dramatic presentation for the children of Woody Vale. Their presentations should:
    1. Present at least four different thinking skills from the worksheet.
    2. Present at least four different aspects of learning styles and preferences from the worksheet.
    3. Communicate the idea that thinking and learning lead to life dreams coming true.
    4. Use mime, tableau and/or silent role play: they must not include any speaking.
    5. Last no more than two minutes.
● Ensure that the children understand the difference between thinking skills and learning styles (learning styles would be

working alone, writing, listening, sitting still and so on; thinking skills would include cooperation, creative thinking, problem-solving).

Drawing together

● Ask the groups to take it in turns to perform their dramas to the rest of the class.
● Video or photograph each performance, with appropriate permissions.
● Tell audience groups to try to identify which aspects from the Learning tableau worksheet are being shown.
● Assess each performance against the criteria set. Questions to consider: *Have you clearly presented four learning and four thinking skills? Have you shown some skills that will make your dreams come true? Does the performance last under two minutes? Does it only include mime, tableau or silent role play?*

Support

● Less confident learners could express aspects of learning and thinking in isolation, without making any connection to their future aspirations.
● Group less confident learners with those who are more confident or who have a deeper understanding of thinking and learning skills.

Extension

● Replay the recorded dramas and ask children to assess them against the success criteria, making suggestions for how the performances could be developed.
● Challenge children to create a storyboard of each performance and ask them to add captions.
● Invite children to create a learning and thinking drama that includes speech.

Painting by numbers

Setting the context
The artwork in hotels is often dull and boring. School art is much more imaginative and inspiring and the international hotel chain, Hotel Spin, knows this. They have asked the pupils in your school to produce original artwork for each one of their 10,000 hotel rooms.

But they have some tough requirements for you to meet – among other curious requests, the artwork must all be the same size and have a 1cm border around it.

The challenge
Create original art using an ideas grid.

Objectives
To recognise the value of teamwork by contributing to a whole-class project.
To explore how to create original artwork to set criteria.

You will need
A wide range of art materials including glitter, paint, coloured pens, photographs, newspapers, colour supplements, coloured card and shapes to draw around (circles, triangles, squares, rectangles and hexagons); copies of photocopiable page 88; a dice for each child.

Preparation
Arrange the art materials in a central resource area in the classroom. Try out the 'Ideas grid' beforehand to familiarise yourself with how it works. You may like to copy the 'Levels of success' chart opposite onto a flipchart or whiteboard, to refer to at the end of the lesson.

Solving the problem
● Share the scenario with the children. The scenario indicates that there are some 'curious' specifications from Hotel Spin: do

the children have any ideas about what these could be?
● Demonstrate the Ideas grid in action. Follow the step-by-step guide on the worksheet to reveal the elements to be included in a piece of artwork. Two throws of the dice will reveal one element. (You need to throw the dice twelve times in order to find the six elements that must be included in your artwork.) An element could be anything from glitter or paint to an ellipsis or five punctuation marks.
● Share the following criteria from Hotel Spin and ensure that the children are able to refer to this throughout the activity:
   1. All artwork should be A4 size with a 1cm white border.
   2. All artwork should include the Hotel Spin logo.
   3. All artwork should include six randomly chosen features from the 'Ideas grid' (chosen by throwing the dice), see photocopiable page 88.
● Set the children to work on the task: give time parameters as required.

Drawing together

● Display the finished pieces of artwork and, as a class, identify the elements from the Ideas grid that have been included in each picture.

● Refer to the 'Levels of success' chart below if desired.

● Discuss the children's experiences of the task. Did they enjoy the project? Did they find it helpful having some guidance as to what the artwork should include or did they find it restrictive?

● Did any of the children encounter problems? For example, what happened if the dice lead to six elements that were all very similar (different coloured card, for example)? How did they make their artwork interesting in this case? Did any children find they had to include features that they didn't want? How did they deal with this? Did anyone cheat and ignore the decisions made by the dice?

Support

● Reduce the possibilities on the grid.

● Suggest ways of dealing with collage (making simple patterns or drawing an outline of a object, such as a house, and using the other elements to decorate it).

Extension

● Adapt the ideas on the grid to include new materials such as fabrics.

● Restrict the resources available so that children have to be more creative in the way that they use them (for example, reduce the number of colours).

● Adapt Hotel Spin's requirements – ask children to make a bigger picture, or a picture that suits a particular room.

Page
85

Levels of success

Not there yet ☆	Nearly there ☆☆	Fantastic ☆☆☆
✔ Artwork not A4	✔ A4 page nearly filled	✔ Artwork is A4
✔ Border missing	✔ Border or logo missing	✔ Border and logo present
✔ Logo missing	✔ Used 3–5 features chosen by the dice	✔ Used 6 features chosen by the dice
✔ Used 3 or fewer features chosen by the dice	✔ Artwork nearly finished	✔ Artwork finished
✔ Artwork not finished		

What's the score?

Sound	Who	When and What
		✗ ✗ ✗ ✗ ✗ ✗ ✗ ✗ ✗
ah		
ooh		
		✗ ✗ ✗ ✗ ✗ ✗ ✗ ✗
ssss		

Learning tableau

| look | talk | move around | be on my own | be hot | be in the dark |

| organise | create | solve problems | ask questions | remember | decide |

| take risks | accept change |

| cooperate |

| listen | write | sit still | be with others | be cold | be in the light |

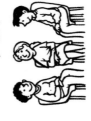  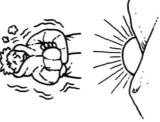 

Ideas grid

6	Glitter	Photo of object	Red pen	Blue pen	Green pen	Orange pen
5	Blue card	Card (any 1 colour)	Photo of animal	Pen (any 1 colour)	Faces	Red paint
4	Green paint	Paint (any 1 colour)	Yellow card	Glitter	Photo of a person	5 printed punctuation marks
3	Blue pencil	Photo of an animal	Hexagons	5 printed nouns	Blue paint	Thought bubbles
2	Circles	Squiggles	5 printed adjectives	Rectangles	5 printed adverbs	Triangles
1	5 printed verbs	5 printed capital letters	Squares	5 printed pronouns	Ellipses	Doors
	1	**2**	**3**	**4**	**5**	**6**

How to use the grid

You need to throw a six-sided dice twice to reveal what element you must include in your artwork.

1. Throw the dice, look at the number facing upwards and move your finger that many squares across the numbers at the bottom of the grid.

2. Throw the dice again. Move from the number at the bottom of the grid, upwards, counting the number of squares shown on the dice.

3. Whatever you find in that square, you must include in your artwork. For example, a throw of 4, then 3 means you have to include five printed nouns in your artwork.

4. Repeat steps 1–3 to select five more elements to include in your artwork.

Illustration © 2008 Moreno Chiacchiera

Chapter Six

Thinking, learning and PE

- Bigger, better
  all-team rounders   90
- Virtual helpers   92

This chapter provides opportunities for children to develop their thinking and learning skills in the context of PE.

- All-team rounders is an adaptation of the standard rounders game and was introduced in the book, *Creative Activities: Thinking and Learning Skills 5–7*. **Bigger, better all-team rounders** takes the game a stage further, by introducing new objects for the children to incorporate into the game, from musical instruments and balloons to toys and even a dictionary! Children are encouraged to think creatively and evaluate their new versions of the game, discussing what worked, what didn't and why.

- In **Virtual helpers**, children develop their knowledge of different sports and creative thinking skills by exploring how their virtual helpers, in this case sports people and a range of sports equipment, can help them to solve problems. Children work independently or in small groups to find solutions to a scenario of a swarm of bees which have escaped from their hive. They then discuss their ideas and are encouraged to come together as a whole class to create a list of their solutions and then decide among themselves which are the best ones.

Bigger, better all-team rounders

Setting the context
Normal rounders can get quite boring what with all that standing around waiting to bat or wondering if the ball will ever come your way. You might already have played all-team rounders which is much better. In this game, the whole batting team runs around following the batter on each hit, while all the fielders race to catch the ball, then line up and make a leg tunnel (through which they pass the ball) before the batters make it back to the start. Whichever team shouts out first gets one point. Bigger, better all-team rounders lets you add rules to make the game even more challenging.

The challenge
Creatively add rules to all-team rounders to make the game more demanding and to make players think more tactically.

Objectives
To develop collaboration skills in a team.
To develop strategic and tactical thinking.
To understand and follow basic game rules.

You will need
Five cones; a rounders bat; a tennis ball; lots of balloons; a football; a cymbal and a beater; a dictionary; a teddy bear; a puppet; a digital camera. You may also want children to note their ideas for new rules on copies of photocopiable page 94.

Preparation
Set up a standard rounders pitch and organise the children into two well-matched teams (according to their ability in PE). Prepare a copy of the 'Levels of success' chart to display on a flipchart or whiteboard.

What to do
● Play standard all-team rounders, with the following rules:
1. All-team rounders is similar to normal rounders but there is very little waiting about.
2. The batter gets three chances to hit the ball.
3. When he/she chooses to run, all the other batters must follow him/her in a safe line. Their aim is to all get back to the start.
4. When all the batters have made it back, the last batter raises his/her hand and shouts, 'Batters in!'
5. While the batters are running, all the fielders must run to where the ball has landed.
6. All the fielders must then line up, make a leg tunnel, and pass (or roll) the ball through all their legs, from one end of the tunnel to the other.
7. When the last fielder receives the ball, he/she holds it in the air and shouts, 'Fielders through!'
8. The team that calls first gets one point.
9. The bowler must be changed for each new batter.
10. The game continues until everyone has had a chance to bat and bowl, with teams swapping roles halfway through.
11. Fielders must give way to batters.

- Show children the extra objects that you have collected (the balloon, the cymbal, the puppet, the dictionary and so on).
- Ask children to get into pairs and think up alternative creative activities for the batting and bowling teams. For example: batters must fully inflate (but not tie off) a balloon each; fielders must all become a different word from the dictionary beginning with 'F' and line up in alphabetical order; batters must take it in turns to hit the cymbal with the stick, passing it along their line; fielders must take a digital photograph of themselves posing as a team.
- Choose alternative activities and try them out, bearing safety in mind.

Drawing together
- Bring the children back together.
- Compare the new batter and fielder activities to the original ones.
- Try playing new versions of the game and evaluate how well the children are using the success criteria. Some ideas may not work at all. If this is the case, discuss why they don't work. *Are there any conclusions that can be made or advice we can give to anyone wanting to invent a game?*
- Consider safety issues for all scenarios.

Support
- Adapt the game and play it in smaller teams.
- Suggest alternative batter and fielder actions according to the skills and maturity of the children.

Extension
- Challenge more confident learners to devise a rounders-style game that involves three equal-sized teams playing at once – what might the third team be doing?
- Change the size of the bat, the ball, the pitch or the cones.
- Add further creative objects for children to incorporate into their new version of rounders.

Levels of success

Not there yet ☆	Nearly there ☆☆	Fantastic ☆☆☆
✔ Not enjoyable to play	✔ Some children enjoyed it	✔ Everyone enjoyed it
✔ Not everyone was involved	✔ Most children were involved	✔ Everyone was involved
✔ Too simple or too complicated	✔ Mostly the right level	✔ Challenging but not too difficult to learn

Virtual helpers

Setting the context
The world is full of challenges and problems: just the other day I was walking to school and came across a cat stuck up a tree, a dog that had fallen down an open drain, a bird stuck in a chimney and a hippopotamus wedged under a bridge. Fortunately, I knew how to solve all of these problems. You only need two things to solve a problem: belief that you can do it and a strategy to help you do it. Belief depends on how you are feeling and a strategy can be learned. My strategy is really easy to learn. All I do is imagine that I have a team of sports people and unlimited sports equipment to help me. I don't really, but when I imagine that I do, I always come up with an idea that I would never have thought of normally. This is called 'off the field' thinking.

The challenge
The Make-Believe Bees have escaped from their hive and are causing trouble. They have settled in my desk drawer! Use a problem-solving strategy to provide a solution.

Objectives
To learn how to apply a creative problem-solving strategy.
To explore applying physical skills and sports equipment to solving a problem.

You will need
Display a bee picture and perhaps also pictures of sports equipment. You could think up some problems in addition to the one suggested.

Preparation
Prepare a very large picture of bees to show to the children at the start of the activity. Make copies of the 'Virtual helpers' worksheet on page 95 (optional).

Solving the problem
● Share the scenario and problem with the children.
● Demonstrate your problem-solving strategy, that you often imagine that you have a team of sports people and a lorry-load of sports equipment when you are confronted with a problem.
● Begin by defining a different problem, for example, a cat is stuck up a tree. Write down some initial solutions such as: call the fire brigade; get a ladder; call to the cat; tempt it down with some food.
● Introduce some virtual sports helpers who will have additional skills and therefore offer ideas. For example: a gymnast could swing up and grab the cat; a climber could

use ropes and other equipment to climb up and get the cat; a runner perhaps one who runs marathon races for charity...) could dress up as a dog and run towards the tree very fast to scare it down.

● Introduce virtual sports equipment to stimulate further ideas. For example: use a cricket net to catch the cat; use a tennis racket to hit a ball towards a leafy branch above the cat, the sudden rustling of the leaves will scare it down; squirt some swimming pool water at the cat to make it come down.

● Check that the children understand how to use virtual sports people and virtual sports equipment as starting points to stimulate their creative problem solving.

● Then, introduce the Make-Believe Bees and challenge the children to think alone or in pairs or threes to create at least ten interesting, sports-based solutions to the bee problem.

Drawing together

● After 15 minutes, ask the children to consider the ideas their group or pair has come up with and, on their own, to select the idea that they think is best.

● Each child should share their best idea with someone else or with another small group.

● Bring the children back together and collect and record on a flipchart or whiteboard the best ideas the children have heard.

● Ask the children to choose which of these 'best ideas' is their favourite and why.

● Record their choices and reasons given.

● Suggest to the children that the reasons given (*It's funny; It's simple; It's clever* and so on) are very good criteria for spotting excellent ideas.

● Explain that they should remember these criteria when problem-solving again and that you will use the list created in class to help you spot their good ideas in the future.

Support

● Limit the choice of virtual helpers and equipment or provide a list of ideas as starting points.

● Choose a different problem to solve.

Extension

● Remind children to apply the strategy to other problems and encourage them to develop it and make it their own: they could use virtual helpers from different disciplines (business, construction, science and so on) and the related virtual equipment (computers, tools, chemicals).

Bigger, better all-team rounders

- Use the equipment provided to think of four new rules for All-team rounders.

Rules for batters:
(Example: Batters must fully inflate (but not tie off) a balloon each.)

1. _____

2. _____

Rules for fielders:
(Example: Fielders must all become a different word from the dictionary beginning with 'F' and line up in alphabetical order.

1. _____

2. _____

- Which is the best new rule the class has come up with?

- Explain why.

How to keep safe:

_____

_____

Virtual helpers

- How could sports people and their equipment help you to remove the escaped bees from the desk drawer and return them to their hive? Think of at least ten ideas and list them below.

1.	
2.	
3.	
4.	
5.	
6.	
7.	
8.	
9.	
10.	

- Which is your favourite idea?

  Explain why.

_____

_____

_____

_____

_____

Illustration © 2008 Moreno Chiacchiera

PHOTOCOPIABLE *Creative Activities for Thinking and Learning Skills: Ages 7–11*

In this series:

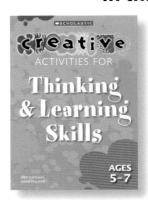

ISBN 978-1407-10005-0

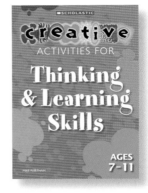

ISBN 978-1407-10006-7

Also available:

Shortlisted for the EDUCATIONAL RESOURCES AWARDS 2005

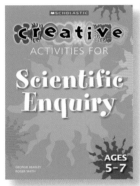

ISBN 978-0439-94500-4

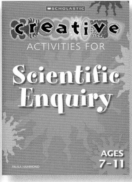

ISBN 978-0439-94501-1

ISBN 978-0439-97111-9

ISBN 978-0439-97112-6

ISBN 978-0439-97113-3

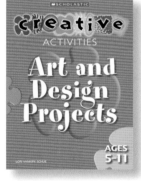

ISBN 978-0439-96526-2

ISBN 978-0439-96525-5

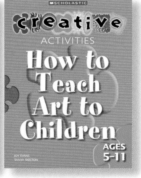

ISBN 978-0439-96524-8

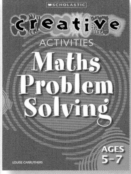

ISBN 978-0439-96556-9

ISBN 978-0439-96570-5

Available for Scotland:

ISBN 978-1407-10088-3

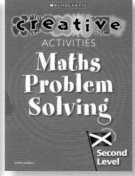

ISBN 978-1407-10089-0

ISBN 978-1407-10060-9

ISBN 978-1407-10061-6

To find out more, call: 0845 603 9091 or visit our website www.scholastic.co.uk